From God To You: Absolute Truth

I am,
You are,
We are one

You will truly be amazed.
You are beginning the journey of your lifetime.
The journey into God, into self!

Elliott Eli Jackson

4880 Lower Valley Road, Atglen, Pennsylvania 19310

Young Stars Sculpt Gas with Powerful Outflows in the Small Magellanic Cloud © NASA, ESA,and A. Nota (STScI/ESA)

Schiffer Books are available at special discounts for bulk purchases for sales promotions or premiums. Special editions, including personalized covers, corporate imprints, and excerpts can be created in large quantities for special needs. For more information contact the publisher:

Schiffer Publishing Ltd.
4880 Lower Valley Road
Atglen, PA 19310
Phone: (610) 593-1777
Fax: (610) 593-2002
E-mail: Info@schifferbooks.com

For the largest selection of fine reference books on this and related subjects, please visit our web site at **www.schifferbooks.com**

We are always looking for people to write books on new and related subjects. If you have an idea for a book please contact us at the above address.

This book may be purchased from the publisher. Include $5.00 for shipping. Please try your bookstore first. You may write for a free catalog.

In Europe, Schiffer books are distributed by:

Bushwood Books
6 Marksbury Ave.
Kew Gardens
Surrey TW9 4JF England
Phone: 44 (0) 20 8392-8585
Fax: 44 (0) 20 8392-9876
E-mail: info@bushwoodbooks.co.uk
Website: www.bushwoodbooks.co.uk

Copyright © 2010 by Elliott Eli Jackson
Library of Congress Control Number: 2009936374

All rights reserved. No part of this work may be reproduced or used in any form or by any means—graphic, electronic, or mechanical, including photocopying or information storage and retrieval systems—without written permission from the publisher.

The scanning, uploading and distribution of this book or any part thereof via the Internet or via any other means without the permission of the publisher is illegal and punishable by law. Please purchase only authorized editions and do not participate in or encourage the electronic piracy of copyrighted materials.

"Schiffer," "Schiffer Publishing Ltd. & Design," and the "Design of pen and ink well" are registered trademarks of Schiffer Publishing Ltd.

Designed by Stephanie Daugherty
Type set in Lithos Pro /New Baskerville BT
ISBN: 978-0-7643-3469-6
Printed in the United States of America

Dedication

For Diane Marie
My love, my joy, my teacher,
the one who has given me
heaven on Earth.

You found me still lost,
downtrodden, and broken.
Unable to give and receive love
in the romantic realm,
You reintroduced me to life.

For life is love and love is life!
Therefore, I dedicate this book to you,
My love, my life, my wife!

Acknowledgments

First and foremost, I would like to thank You, God, the source of all, She/He, the beginning and the end, the motivating factor within all things seen and unseen, explained and unexplained, that which is the flow, the force of life as we know it on Earth and in Heaven, with all its intricacies and complexities.

Diane, who has transcribed most of the information channeled from above, is the one who woke me each day to work on this important piece and whose heart sustained my mind and hands as I wrote. [What is offered to the world now].

I desire to acknowledge my parents, Harold and Florastein Jackson, who taught me to love and give of self. My mother would watch me from the window as I played in the streets. She knew one day this book would come. She knew I was here to give truth one day; it is the reason my friends laughed at her watching me at every turn. It is the reason she would call me overseas just before I engaged in some activity of low vibration and say, "Son, don't do it!" As for my father, in all my travels I have not as yet met a human on this Earth such as he is. He would literally never say "no" to another human being's request.

Neale Donald Walsch, for your bravery and vision. I, along with millions of others have come to remember much because of you. Oprah Winfrey, a woman of courage that I believe still does not know the effect she had on this humble man. And Esther and Jerry Hicks, the vanguards of Collective and Mass Consciousness; without you many would not understand at all.

The men who stuck by me when I was most assuredly out of control, Michael Perry, Emanuel Purvis, Ricky Gibson, and David Goodwin. My sister, Harolyn, and her husband, Lubbie Williams, for holding me up during dark days. My children, Shanee, Elliott, and Adrianna, who gave me reason and purpose to continue life.

Beverly Ann Wilson, Kay Elana Wagnon, Neal Harris. These wonderful people gave me insights into my spiritual God self. And the late Rev. H.S. Malone and Al Boswell, the two men who told me at an early age that I had something to tell the world that would come directly from the SOURCE of all.

Bono ... who loves the world.

John Lennon ... for seeing.

Al Gore ... who is not afraid to speak.

Michael Jackson ... for his music and the pure love in his being, misunderstood as he was, in his actions.

Arnold Schwarzenegger ... a man not afraid to take action.

Kudos to Deepak Chopra, the Dalai Lama, Dr. Wayne Dyer, Marianne Williamson, Dr. Phillip C. McGraw (Dr. Phil), Maya Angelou, Ben Stein, Barack Obama, Tony Lindsay, Max Lucado, Hillary Rodham Clinton, Louise L. Hay, Bob Dylan, A.S. Byatt, M. Scott Peck, Marvin Meyer, Joyce Meyer, Thomas Moore, Stephen King, Toni Morrison, The Foundation For Inner Peace, William Shakespeare, Edgar Cayce, and Kahlil Gibran. These men and women, along with many unnamed and unremembered as of yet, have or have had the ability to show us the scope of the magnificent mind we all have and can use to remember who we are. And there are many, many more capable of setting forth great works and accomplishments. All these things are possible and plausible for them and for you, too. For we are One, so acknowledgments go to all on Planet Earth and beyond, whoever you are, wherever you are, whatever you do, and however you do it.

For the cover artwork: Andrea Theocles gives new meaning to the word expressionism. Life changing experiences opened her up to a higher visionary vibration. Andrea invites the observers to travel into her world of color and emotion, to share the subtle universal messages that have the potential to open their hearts and minds. She attempts to evoke the deep stirrings of love and passion that is inside all of us and tries to go one step beyond to a higher plane of feeling through color and a sense of movement.

Across distance,
time and space,
Our souls have once again
come to this
Magnificent Place!

Contents

	Note to Reader	10
	Author's Preface	12
	Poem — Once Again	17
	Introduction	19
I	Who We Are, Who You Are	23
II	Life as We Understand It	37
III	Death	44
IV	The Physical Body — What's Good, What's Not	53
V	Love of Self and Others: Relationships	65
VI	Spiritual Realms: Angels and Such	85
VII	The Path of Least Resistance	108
VIII	Priorities	113
IX	Other Planets, Galaxies, and the Inhabitants	152
	Conclusion	158

Diane found something miraculous occurring during meditation. Her husband, Elliott Jackson, spoke the following words:

"I am, you are, we are one."

In my quiet living room, the words spoken through my husband's vocal cords both surprised and shocked me. The thought occurred to me that he was kidding around. However, within a short period of time I knew without a shadow of a doubt that the energy and words coming through him were from another source outside of him. There was something different, enchanting, about his eyes and his voice. I realized that my Elliott was not conscious or present as usual.

In my shock and amazement, I was temporarily rendered speechless. The next words spoken were, "We are here for you; you have questions, we have answers; you may ask us anything you desire."

After regaining my composure, I asked, "Who are you?" The answer came, "We are all that there is, was, and ever shall be; we are love and light and you are love and light." They told me that they were "whom I had prayed to as a child at bedtime" and "whom I had called out to for help during my times of pain, turmoil, and fear." They told me that they were "the beginning and the end of all things or that which I was taught to be God."

Tears of joy began flowing down my face for it was at that exact moment that I realized within the core of my very being the full immensity, power, and love of God. Every question that I had ever asked throughout my lifetime was now being answered — questions in reference to the origin of life, whether or not there existed anything outside of my physical reality, what happens when we die, and if there was something or someone who really listened to me when I prayed. The indescribable joy, peace, and hope that I experienced was overwhelming. That evening, I finally understood with absolute certainty that we are not alone. I finally understood that all people are one with each other and one with a loving being, that which we understand God to be. These truths became indelibly imprinted within my memory.

There were many times when I would awaken during the wee hours of the night to find Elliott at the computer in a semi-conscious state, dazed, automatically typing what would become this book. Once I began reading what was being given to Elliott, I knew that you too would find the same love, peace, and joy, along with renewed hope in life.

Note to Reader

What you are about to read is for all of you, on your home, your planet, your Earth. It is the beginning of a wonderful never-ending session, a continuing session of remembrance. It will open the door to yourself; it will smash the misinformation and lies passed on throughout time, as you understand time to be. Fore, WE have come to tell you the "Absolute Truth."

Many of you think or believe you understand the Truth already. Many of you think you have come to enlightenment. If this is true, WE will see. If you have, you too will read this book, you will not say, I have no need to read those words; I know it all. I am an Ascended Master. Fore, you cannot be ascended until you have returned to US. That is "Absolute Truth." And, of course, if you have returned to US, you would not be reading this or claiming you need not read it.

You also will not judge any, if you have come to high vibration. You will not say the vegetarian knows the way, or only those who pray to the east know the way, or only those who know the Christ, know the way. Fore, there is only one way and it is not through another; it is only through remembrance of who you are, a part of US. You will not judge this work or any other. You will understand that it is from all of you. Everything you do is from all of you. Even your current world economic situation is from all of you.

Most importantly, you would understand that you or another has never done anything wrong. You may have made some poor decisions and taken part in some things that were and are not in your highest good. You will begin to remember when things no longer serve you. And you will move away from them. Fore, know You are all wonderful just as you are.

• Anyone who tells you that you are not wonderful is not a representation of US.

• Anyone who tells you that you are limited in what you can do is not a representation of US.

• Anyone who tells you that you cannot get to US, does not understand that all return to US sooner or later.

Any one of you who understands not, that you have the opportunity each second to change your reality is one not at a high vibration. You can change your reality at any given time. You all have the greatest gift the universe has to offer: freedom of choice. Therefore, choose to renew yourself; remember who you are. Fore, The Time is Now! Know that you would not be reading this unless it was time.

WE LOVE YOU!

Author's Preface

If you have found this book within your hands, it was sent to your subconscious being. It was sent to you so you could read of another one of the miracles of the universe. It is surely a miracle. Not too long ago, just a few years back, I sat in a bathroom, on a toilet with blood running down my arm as I tried frantically to place the needle within my vein to feel the heroin, to feel nothing of life. All of this happened as my son knocked on the door pleading for his father to let him in. I wanted to die, to fly somewhere, anywhere except my own skin. But no matter how hard I tried, I would not die. Now I know why! What you are reading was given to me by, as they call themselves, WE, or if you like, God, as each of us understands God to be.

Therefore this book, to be politically correct or up-to-date in current verbiage, is divinely inspired. It is the result of what is termed to be automatic typing. Unbeknownst to me, I would arise from bed at the very early hour of two or three in the morning, or so I have been told by my wife. At approximately six or seven in the morning, I would find myself sitting at my desk in front of the computer with pages upon pages of typed material completed.

It is important first for you to know who I am, or better still, who I was. I was a person lost, as are many of us. I say lost because I had no real direction or purpose. I began using drugs at the age of thirteen. I do not come from a broken home, I was not abused. I have no tale of a messed up childhood. I picked the life I lived; now I choose another, as can all of us.

For twenty-two years or so, I lived in the drug culture. I appeared to be okay at face value. I worked, shopped, married, and traveled the world. Yet, each day, I woke up high and depressed and went to bed high and depressed. I lived to get just one more substance in me, any substance. The substances I used were many: marijuana, cocaine, heroin, acid and the like, even food— anything I could get my hands on. It did not matter what I had to do to get them or who I hurt in the process. I also gave myself to any and every woman I could. I was drowning in a sea of confusion and did not care. I was married at the early age of twenty-one and shipped overseas to England to serve a country I did not believe in or respect. I was a mess. I cheated on my unsuspecting loving wife and neglected my children. I worked hard to give my money to others. I played even harder. I had moments of clarity and joy but they were all short lived. I was bitter and hateful masking it with jokes and smiles as many of us do or have done.

My loving parents gave all they could in support of me, though I did not appreciate their love or support. I was a shell of a man. I was hopeless and useless to myself and the world. I had given up on mankind and myself.

There *was* somewhere deep inside me, however, hope. There was the hope I heard from my mother as a child, the hope I saw each time my father would go way beyond his means to pull me out of a jam, the hope I saw in the old women's faces in church. In the midst of what I thought to be a world of pure corruption, I always made it out kind of untouched.

How? I've been hunted like a dog by drug dealers for pulling moves on them. I've stood right next to drug dealers after spending days with them and they knew not who I was, as they looked for me. How did I escape? I sold myself and all I had or all that others had if I could get my hands on it. I allowed myself to be hit and spat upon to get more drugs. I put myself in situations I would not put my worst enemy in. I would ask myself each night as I would come out of a stupor: Why oh, why was I still alive?

Well now I know why. I stopped using drugs after many attempts to do so. I began to listen to my inner self and others who had hope. Then I began to help others; I found a passion, a place in this world. However, there was something still missing; I did not know what. I could not put my hands on it. While cleaning myself up, I became a therapist and addiction counselor. I went on to do motivational speaking, gained some success or so I thought. I put together over twenty years of assisting others in their attempts to stop using drugs and obtain a higher level of consciousness.

Then, in 2005, something happened. I began to write poetry. I didn't even like poetry; I thought it for fools and overly sensitive people. To top it off, I had not written any prior to that year. Further, I had no interest in writing poetry. Amazingly, over 500 poems poured from my being in less than a year. I wrote poems on life, love, lost love, pain, and spirit. I wrote poem after poem after poem. They just would not stop coming. I had hundreds of pieces of paper everywhere with titles on them. I became consumed, better still, obsessed with writing. I stopped working and began to devote all of my time and effort to putting together a book of poetry.

So in 2006, *Cacophony* was born, a collection of ninety-two poems which received critical acclaim. I was published in various anthologies throughout the United States and Europe. My poems started being featured in Art Galleries, selling at prices ranging up to $175 a poem. On the internet *Cacophony* consistently received only five-star ratings from customers and was somehow paired with Louise Hay's ground-breaking book, *You Can Heal Your Life*.

And I did not understand why any of this was happening. See, I was of the firm belief that man was alone in this vast universe and I did not subscribe to the notion of divinely inspired information or any angelic help.

All this changed in early 2007.

On a summer night in our quiet living room in Illinois, something miraculous occurred. You see, my wife, Diane, talked me into going to a channeling class, at (let us say) her unrelenting insistence. I did not want to go; my training in counseling and my sense of logic told me it would be a total waste of time and run by a charlatan out to get our hard-earned monies.

I was cautious, yet curious, as to what channeling involved. We decided to approach the class with an open mind. We had little expectation that anything would occur during the first practice meditation we were assigned to do. To my wife's shock and amazement, so I am told, I spoke the words "I am, you are, we are one. We are here for you, you have questions, we have answers; you may ask us anything you desire."

After she regained her composure she asked, "Who are you?" The answer came, "We are all that there is, was, and ever shall be, we are love and light and you are love and light." They told her that they were "whom she had prayed to as a child at bedtime" and "whom she had called out to for help during her times of pain, turmoil, and fear." They told her that they were "the beginning and the end of all things or that which she was taught to be God." Or, as they prefer to be called, "All there is, was, and ever shall be," and that they would begin to "speak verbally through me to her and later to others."

During this occurrence, my wife tells me I spoke of things that I could have no knowledge or understanding of and that I appeared to be in a semi-conscious state. Diane informed me that she was surprised and skeptical at first, thinking it was a joke, as I have been known for kidding around.

She told me that after several minutes of listening, tears of joy began to flow down her face. It was at this point that she realized that it was no joke. God was real and speaking directly to her. When I came to, I found her crying. She informed me of what had occurred. We have never been the same since that night. Everything we have done since that time has been motivated to help others and ourselves obtain the best in life.

The next time I fell into this state, Diane began to take notes, and soon after began recording most sessions — pages upon pages of information about mankind's history and future resulted. After a few months of daily sessions, I began to rise from bed in the middle of the night and automatically type. The words given to me over a seven-month period are contained within this book. The words are as I now fully embrace and understand divinely inspired from the source of life, or what we understand God to be. As information began to unfold to Diane during sessions, it was revealed that the over 500 poems I wrote were sent to my subconscious mind as an introduction to *From God to You: Absolute Truth*.

Now my lips and voice are used to speak to others and my hands are used to prepare words for you and others to read. Diane, as mentioned, has many volumes of handwritten material and many recorded tapes full of the information given to her through me. Some of it has been used in this manuscript. The rest will be in the four books to follow this one. The only conclusion I can come up with is that what you are about to read is what could be termed, "a result of unconscious production."

When all this began, I was robotic in appearance and speech when they came. Diane would have to follow me around the house, sometimes up to one hour. I would be disorientated and unaware of where I was, or what I was doing. It has progressed to a steady flow of wondrous words and facts of life and joy. I speak these words to many now, crowds come, people call to hear what comes from me, yet not from me.

Many of the passages in this book are short and simple to understand. Some of the passages are very long and what I consider to be boring and tedious, full of unnecessary verbiage. Many words and ideas are repeated several times. Diane, of course, inquired of the WE why this book of information was being transmitted to humanity at this time. Further, she questioned them as to why many portions of the book are repeated, or are seemingly very long and tedious. She was informed that, "The time is now for mankind to hear and listen to these truths from the universe, and the time is now for the reconnection to God as you understand him or her to be and self. All of the material presented in this book is necessary; that what may seem unnecessary to many may not be to others, and everything presented has reason and purpose for all of us."

My personal beliefs or disbeliefs are unimportant. I was, through Diane, directed to publish this manuscript as given without deviation unless told otherwise. We were informed to begin core focus groups across the country, to get a feel on the views of others, how they viewed what has been written and we have done so. Through questions from others, some sections were added to, changed, or clarified by the source of this material. Saying all of this, I submit to you *From God to You: Absolute Truth* for your reading and edification. Many will find this book the beginning of a remembrance process; some will find it at their current mind set, total nonsense. I, of course, have no control over whatever outcome it has on the individual. I have been informed that "Freedom of choice is the greatest gift that we have."

> **Author Note:** Most of the poems were written prior to the transmissions from "All there is, was, and ever shall be," for this book. But there are specific poems that were written by THEM through the automatic transmission process for this book.

Once Again

Once again, we wait.
We wait to begin, once again.
We wait in the place of light, of love.

We wait in the place void of outside influences,
Void of judgments.
Void of predetermined
inoculated poisonous stands or views.

Void of FEAR!
Here we stand,
Once again!
Here we stand before contributions are introduced.
Contributions from human mother,
From human father,
Those contributions that will introduce our DNA,
Our basic molecular structure,
Those genes and cells,
That will twist and turn and divide to
give rise to our up-and-coming physical forms.
Give rise to the Misinformation and Prejudices.
Give rise to Impatience and Intolerance.
Give rise to Hate, Deceit, and Misinterpretations.
Misinterpretations and misquotes of the pure messages
     from the All,
Misinterpretations that will taint our very existence,
Until we remember,
Once again,
Who we are.

So, we wait!
A number impossible to calculate,
Impossible to even consider.

We wait in this place,
This place of pure light and pure love.

This station at which we are docked,
this port, safe within the bosom of the All.
This heavenly cell with no worries,
no stress,
no pain. Only joy and peace!

We mix within the totality of the All.
So, once again we wonder, what form?
We ponder what shape,
What purposes this time?
What manifestations of form will be ours?
What reoccurring faces and places will appear?
What countries will be revisited?
Unpredictable to us,
in our shapeless forms.
Nothing new to these old souls.
We, travelers of this universe,
travelers of this cosmos,
travelers of time, distance, and space.
Travelers having traversed this course before.
Many times before.

So once again, Mother Earth, will we delight in the sight
of your blue skies?
Once again, shall we breathe the sweet fragrances
    of your flowers,
And inhale your dust and dirt?
We shall once again feel the caress of your sea breeze
    upon our faces.
So, once again, after dancing, floating in freedom
from constraints of the physical,
freedom from the cumbersome
restrictive movement of human manifestation,
once again shall we obtain the chance to correct?
To learn from the past?
To remember those lessons not mastered before?
In anticipation we wait.
Once again.

INTRODUCTION

Almost all my entire adult life I was hopelessly trapped in some kind of self-defeating destructive behavior. This life of mine has consisted of periods of low self-esteem and self-doubt covered by a mask of confidence. This was my secret. When I finally did begin to step outside the grip of fear, I began to help and assist others, those trying to end many of the same destructive behaviors that I had practiced for many years.

Silently, I would curse that which I thought or considered to be God for my lot in life. I very rarely did this publicly. Most of the time I would, shall I say, act as if I bought into the beliefs that there was a God. Those beliefs placed upon me, those taught to me. I did not believe in this God, nor feel that old-time religion. I did, of course, as most who are unhappy, blame that which I had no faith in. I refused to believe that it was I who created how my life had turned out, somewhat successful but not happy by any stretch of the imagination. I was lost, bewildered, and confused. Not in my wildest dreams or imagination did I think the events of the past two years could or would happen to me or anyone else. I did, however, have a small thread of hope that God truly existed; a little thought that there was something out there bigger and wiser than I was.

Despite all of this, I am now being used by the universe, through this book and in other ways. I serve others and self today, thinking of what is in my highest good and the highest good of others. It is time for you to do this also. Each of us are called from deep within our being to have the best this life has to offer and assist others in obtaining the same.

This book contains simple truths, answers to those things that I and most others question all of our lives. Now I know without a shadow of a doubt that these truths are of love. Truths, which if followed or adhered to, can revolutionize our life and change our existence. You may now and forever have a positive life full of love, hope, and joy.

So right here, right now, you too are either starting or continuing the journey towards God and Self. It is a wonderful journey that you have always been on, yet many of us did not realize or acknowledge it. Many people, as I did, thought happiness to be the secret of a few or unattainable for us; but it is not. The journey or path to a higher vibration is for all. It lies within all of us, this path to abundance and prosperity. All that is required is to follow your inner voice and the words you are about to read.

These words were given to me from the Source of All things; they were channeled through me to Diane on many occasions and also inserted within my memory. I was told that on a certain date I would begin writing and I did. I was instructed to become ready for a crash course in Biochemistry, Physics, Bioscience and the holographic universe, subjects that I knew very little about, had no concern for, and personally thought I did not LIKE. I was further instructed to look into the misquoting of Jesus. I did such.

So with all this said, it does not matter if you believe or disbelieve what I have written. It is not my concern. I was instructed to write these words, to publish this book, and make it available for use by my fellow man. I know not what will happen after completion, but man oh man, the All loves US so much. The following are the words of YOU — ME— and if you like, GOD!

From The Source of All Life

YOU stand at a juncture, a crossroad in human endeavor and human history. The mass consciousness of your planet is shifting, changing, evolving, and you are a part of it. It began long ago in earlier civilizations. There have always been some seekers, some searchers, the ones laughed at, persecuted, and even killed for thinking of and saying things that were not accepted at a particular time by the masses, or approved by the ones given power by the masses, whichever the case may have been.

These ones started revolutions, affected change, rounded out the Earth from its known state. They have given you music to calm your soul, art to please your eyes. They have contributed much towards the advancement of your home, your Earth. These ones also looked up at the stars in the sky and knew, just knew, there was more than meets the eye. These are the ones who were able to reach a higher vibrational level in thought and action. As can YOU!

Men such as Plato, Newton, Beethoven, Einstein, Columbus, Edwin Land, William Randolph Hearst, Jesus, Aristotle, and Napoleon Bonaparte, along with women such as Gargi, a philosopher, Pan Chao, a scholar in the court of the Emperor Ho, Martha Logan, horticulturalist, Acca Laurentia, a healer, Aganice, the one who computed the positions of the planets in the court of Pharaoh Sesotris, Sophia Pereyaslaw, marine biologist, and Ruth Benedict who helped shape anthropology. Many of these women are little known to many of you. Yet you need to know that they were all guided by the All. Each was given divine insight into matters of life, of death, and of hope and joy. You too are given such each day! You, the inventors of fire, electricity, glass, silk, and the simple way mothers change a diaper, all of this information has come to you from the All. The genius in each and every one of you comes from the All. You who are endogenous were brought out of the caves and dark dwellings you lived in and were educated by the All. All you have done on your planet, the knowledge of decimal notations and the idea of the computer came from the All, OUR gifts to Ourselves.

And most recently, individuals, such as those mentioned in the acknowledgement of this book, have been able to touch the minds and hearts of so many. People all over your globe are waking up and standing up for this simple truth, "We Are ONE. There never has and will never be any disconnection from the Source of it All. Every person you know, all the drivers of the cars you pass, the people with whom you interact with on a daily basis are all you and you are them."

But, you already knew this; you felt this, you didn't want anyone to know you knew. You were remembering who you were. You were remembering from whence you came since that first question in your mind about what you were taught at home and in schools in reference to how all of that which you know began. Since the first time you asked, "Why is a particular event or thing occurring? Why must I be limited in my life on any level? Why financially, mentally, or even romantically am I stagnated? Or maybe you just asked yourself, why am I here?"

Actually, the truth has been told to you and all others throughout time. Every generation has been privy to it. However, most of you have just chosen not to hear, not to believe. For, to many of you, it is just too simple. And so it is with many. The one writing this book was one who also did not believe in his inner self, his inner thoughts, that maybe, just maybe, he could be able to heal others, even himself; that he could talk directly to God, and just maybe, that he could be like that Walsch guy or Benny Hinn or even Jesus? WE tell you this, all of you can.

Of course, then came the fearful thoughts that he couldn't tell anyone, he would be labeled, branded an outcast, jeered at, laughed at. He would have no friends. He would end up alone, on his own. Well, he was quite wrong as are many of you. Now there are Millions and Millions of seekers, of people just like him reaching a higher vibrational level, healing themselves and the world.

Join them! They will show you how. They are not a cult, not a fad. They are not a bunch of loonies running around using witchcraft and heresy, or even non-conformity.

They are humans, just as you. Yet they are displacing the myths and confusion. Yes, sensible, reliable informed people, who have changed perceptions and are remembering, are no longer willing to be silent. They will be vocal to the fact that WE are ALL ONE, and that each of you can be trained to heal yourselves and others.

Be encouraged that there are many doctors who are taking a Holistic viewpoint in their practices. They should be commended by you. Many doctors are remembering the fact that sounds and vibrations can retrain the body and the mind to uplift itself, that meditation is the first step to higher mentality and total wellbeing.

So within the contained pages of this book, information has been placed for your use and dissemination to help all of you remember who you are. What is given here to you as you read are ideas to stimulate the remembrance process. What is given here is given for the changing of perceptions and ideas that all of you knew were possible and true, but did not believe were valid due to poor previous instructions and teachings. WE have hidden from plain site (on purpose) between the words, extra messages, and connections that are not seen by the naked eye, yet will be understood by the subconscious mind and the highest vibration of the human spirit. Therefore, WE begin at the beginning.

I

Who We Are, Who You Are

"I did not believe any of this was possible, yet it is. Thus, given to me these words:"

One of the most important facts for you to know and to understand is that the writer of this book is YOU. All of YOU, for you are US and WE are YOU. The vehicle WE are using to present this material to you at this time is Elliott. He is only a representation of all of you. Do not allow his gender or the color of his skin to cause disregard for what is being put forth to you. Do not allow his past behaviors or past decisions to cause a disregard either, for all of you have also transgressed against your wonderful selves.

Grasp the idea that at each moment of what you understand to be a new day, each of you has the absolute right to create yourself anew. Know that whenever any of you speak or act with your highest good in mind or the highest good of others, it is US. Whenever any of you inspire others or yourself, it is US. Therefore, all of you at one time or another were and are being used by US to give the absolute truth, hope, and joy to others. You do this to help uplift them and yourselves.

Contrary to the popular beliefs held by most of you and handed down in lore, all which you know did not start in a fairytale setting. Additionally, the explanations that many scientists give are very close, but miss the mark somewhat. It is time to set the story and record straight for all of humanity. WE will not allow you to live in darkness any longer; it is time for you to remember who and what you are. Therefore, WE will give the proper information to you, what you do with it is, of course, up to you. The one thing WE do not interfere with is freedom of choice within your realm. It is one of the most important truths in the universe as you know it, and not a trivial matter.

Freedom of choice springs from the love that is All there is. Without it, all would be in vain and all creators would be under totalitarian rule. This is not allowed in any realm. There are, moreover, rules to the cosmos and beyond, rules that will be explained in simple terms so please don't misinterpret this in your simple minds. WE mean "simple" only in the sense that you do not use them to their full capabilities, another choice of yours. So please do not be offended.

From Whence We Came

LOVE!
A soul, your soul, my soul,
all results of LOVE.
Pure LOVE created us.
From the bowels of this universe,
we come.
From the bowels of mother Earth,
we come.
From the bowels of man and woman,
we come.
The deepest self, formed in the
womb, the highest thought, LOVE!
It caused us to be, you and me!

So, as you sit and wonder,
ponder this! You Are LOVE!
Your grandest dreams, your highest
ideas, and fondest goals are LOVE.
It is "WHO YOU ARE."
Love yourself, your Beloved Self!

In The Beginning...

In the beginning, there was not darkness, there was Light and Love. WE are Light, YOU are Light. WE are Love; YOU are Love. In language you understand, the source of All is pure energy, which is pure light. Let us take a look at All there is and ever was. Take the suns or stars as you have named them, the ones that dwell within your known solar systems, then magnify them a billion times and you will be just getting to yet a micro section of the immensity of the power of the All. This Light, this Love, as you call it, was nothing except caring and compassionate, life-giving and sustaining, totally self-sufficient. This light is comprised of trillions and trillions of sections and pieces. WE will use your words here — "every cubic centimeter of space contains energy that equals the total energy of all the matter in the known universe." This energy was all amassed or accumulated together in pure harmony. No space between anything at all. This energy is what and where you come from, nothing else, nothing more.

Now what happened? This is what you wish to know!

This total conscious being US, YOU, WE were together, and in your words — (happy). All of the atoms and molecules that define your physical structure and are the building blocks of all solids, liquids, and gases were all together. But there was no pressure, no force. All was still, tranquil, and satisfied. There was no yearning, no dissatisfaction. Peace and calm reigned supreme. This was reality and eternity. So as it is also, right now!

However, if you could see, you would see that even as all is still, all is moving, moving at a rate and speed you can't conceive. Your scientists know this. There is vibration at all times. As WE vibrated and oscillated, something was going on. WE were thinking, "What would it be like to be apart? What would it be like to have a bigger or larger space between US?" So, it is from this single state of total consciousness that WE, in your words, decided to "divide!"

All souls were as one. However, a multitude of souls wanted to expand and experience a new reality, a different one. Thus the division began, inner and outer space, the cosmos, the universes, the stars and planets were formed. For a soul, all souls, your soul and all you understand are but fragments of the ONE!

Fragments Divide

The dividing of US took millions and millions and millions of years. So it would be advantageous for you, your humankind, to stop working on calculating when it occurred. It is impossible to do so until you return to the All. WE did split into atomic matter, alpha particles, molecules, isotopes, planets, curves, liquids and solids, horizontal and vertical motions, gases, static, density, depths, condensation, crystalline substances, impulse, and momentum. Objects collided and speed and velocity were formed. Electrons and friction with lifting force were developed. Gravitational potential and fields were formulated for the known galaxies and the heavens as you call them.

All of this was completed in the, as you say, twinkling of an eye, yet over time and space. All of the terminologies such as, "atmospheric components" and the around ninety-two primordial biomolecules, many of which you have no knowledge of as of yet. You understand about forty of these. Further, the chemical evolutions of organic molecules are also correct assumptions. WE implanted them within the mind of your learned men. All of these processes happened at once and forever, then and now.

A few years back, WE planted in the mind of one of your planet's sons, Neale Donald Walsch, an elementary explanation to prepare you for the one given to you now. WE needed to get you ready for the fact that you, too, had a part and portion in the development of the worlds as you know them, as did your other brothers and sisters from, what you call, "afar." You were at that time in a non-physical state of being. Now it is time for you to remember that each and every one of you are creators. You, as you know yourself to be, create your own experience, then and now. If you do not find your current experience agreeable with whom you think you are, change it — only you can. Therefore, wrap or surround your minds around the fact that YOU are WE, WE are YOU. The All, US, made a collective decision to split, to explore OURSELVES, the last joint decision WE made together since that time. But we will again make decisions together; the time is coming.

WE are informing you now that all of you in physical form began in one central location. This one location was located in what was known to you as Mesopotamia. This is the place where the human race began, your legacy. From there you started to spread outward. As your humankind moved into different climates and elevations on your Earth, your skin, eyes, nostrils, hair, and features developed or changed to adapt to the particular climates and regions of your planet, where groupings of your kind decided to stake claim to as their new home. This is the full explanation of your ethnic differences, there is no other. Check on or look into the information WE have just related to you. Be sure the information you obtain comes from a reliable source. You should always do this. Most information you have received came from made-up stories.

The answer to the question is all of you in human manifestation come from two. The theories, therefore, of crawling out of the sea and, eventually, standing on two legs are in fact just theories. It did take time for you to evolve from two. Over time the laws of the universe came into effect to assure that inbreeding would have, shall WE say, negative results. Inbreeding was appropriate and necessary in the beginning of your world. However, this practice is not of a high vibration or necessary now. Debate as you wish, it does not matter. It is, of course, your choice. WE would have it no other way! It would be good, as you understand the word "good" to be, to look at the evidence of continued inbreeding.

Self Examination

Please, go to a mirror now or after you have read some of this book. When you get to the mirror know that you are face to face with self. While you are there, ask yourself what you see. WE will tell you what you will see; WE will give you the "Absolute Truth."

You see, as many of your planet's higher vibrational thinkers or persons whom have chosen the profession of studying these matters fully understand, a carbon-based unit. This is what you are. Understand "in a nut shell" you are this carbon-based unit and yet much, much more. You are cells containing appropriately seventy to ninety percent water. A vast portion of your being is oxygen, which forms most of your body mass. Additionally, carbon is the base of your molecules which are organic. You are six basic elements entwined to form that which you understand as your body. Carbon, nitrogen, hydrogen, calcium, oxygen and phosphorus are your ingredients. WE added to your being sodium, magnesium, sulfur, zinc, copper, molybdenum, selenium, chlorine, iodine, fluorine, cobalt, iron, manganese, lead, lithium, aluminum, strontium, silicon, arsenic, bromine, and vanadium in miniscule amounts. You are also tissues formed into organs that carry out certain tasks. You are comprised of ten complex systems that function for your being, your body. These systems are skeletal, muscular, nervous, endocrine, cardiovascular, lymphatic, respiratory, digestive, urinary, and reproductive. This is what you are on a scientific level.

Next, WE will explain in greater detail the breaking up or groupings as they were after the split and how they now stand in the physical and spiritual realms. Some of this information many of you remember; many of you don't as of yet. This information will help you when WE explain some of the groupings many of you have not yet remembered. Additionally, WE transmit to you this message:

"BE YE NOT AFRAID OF THE TRUTH, FOR IT WILL, IN YOUR WORDS 'SET YOU FREE!'"

The Unseen

In Temples, Sanctuaries
and Synagogues,
It has been spoken!
In times of turmoil and revelation,
It has been spoken!
In Cathedrals, Mosques
and Seminaries,
It has been spoken!
During prayer and meditation.
The name, the names,
Feared, Awed, Revered!
Shouted at the highest Mountains,
whispered by the deepest waters,
the name, the names.
When troubled and low,
it has been spoken!
For help, relief, and wisdom
when in pain and grief,
It has been spoken! The name, the names.
Of the Unseen.

Who and What WE Are

There are vibrational levels to your known universe. The highest vibrational level or apex of All things is what you on your planet, your home, your Earth, have given many names to, such as; God or Allah, Jahveh or Jehovah, Elohim, Yahweh, Gaia, Varuna, Mitra-Varuna, Tian, Yama or Vishnu, and Lakshmi or Ishvara or Shiva or Durga or, in Sanskrit, circles called Mandalas, Tai Sui, Avalokiteshvara, Pujongnim, and Kami. All of these came from remembrance, as many of you were trying to put together who you are, where you come from. Your imaginations gave you these names, these titles, to help you towards remembering.

Further to your remembrance has come the vibrational sound that the human voice perceives is closest verbalization to US, or the universe. This sound would be that of "Om." WE inform you now that the proper sound associated to US is that of the following; Aaah-moo-Chee-Chee-Aa...ah. This is the sound that the universe as you understand the universe to be resounds with in recognizing OUR vibration. Simply put, drop the Chee-Chee and state Aaah-moo-Aa...ah, if you wish. It is, of course, up to each one of you, whatever you choose to call US.

WE, that which you call God, have and will always be with your psyche; you cannot escape this fact. There has never been a time in what you understand as history that some concept or thought of US has not been around. WE are part of your human experience. WE are your human experience. When you could not find your way in the dark, you called out to something or someone whom you could not see for help. It was US. When you could not figure out the ways to conquer or overcome some seemingly unattainable task or feat, you called out to US and WE always have and will come whenever or wherever there is pain or suffering as you understand pain and suffering to be.

You knew, within your being, that there was a lack, shall we say, of US in the perpetrators of whatever was happening that was of a negative nature. More importantly, you understood whenever greatness occurred or wondrous unexplained things happened, it was not fully of your own doing. Yes, we have a wonderful relationship if one really looks at it for what it truly is, a collaboration. Yet, if one looks or looked at our relationship as one-sided as has so often occurred, the lopsidedness is apparent and undeniable. When man has put falseness to who WE are or who he is, all sorts of unnecessary and unneeded things take place. WE, therefore, are here to set the record straight.

So WE, that which you have placed these names upon, are the portion of All that is, All that can't be surpassed. It is not possible to measure or count our number. It is unforeseen. WE are in fact in your words "infinite;" WE are transient and yet still permanent. This is to say WE are on OUR way in and out at the same time, ever moving, ever changing, yet remaining the same. WE are that light that would be a most astatine or unstable radioactive chemical element to you, if your now human manifestations were exposed to US in pure form. WE can not be touched. WE are the majority of US that by free choice remain in pure light and love. WE do not falter or flinch.

In one of the great writings WE have given to you, the Christian Bible, WE are explained as close as can be in your human terms as "Father of the Heavenly Lights, who do not change like shifting shadows." WE must add here that "father" is not a proper description of US. It is in your words sexist and discriminatory against the other what you have named "gender." Moreover, to those who call US the Goddess, an equal portion of gender separation and discrimination goes out to you. WE are neither HE nor SHE; WE are HE and SHE. Your Sants of India also came very close in remembrance by emphasizing that God lies far beyond human words and description. They remember that WE can be contacted directly and require no intermediary, even The Avatar, their incarnation of God, such as the Christian Jesus. Please don't feed into the lie that one of you, hear US, has ever been or will ever be more special than the other. Remember this no matter what you have been foretold. When you understand this, you will understand fully what the manifestation known to you as Jesus was really imparting to you. WE will touch upon this later.

Therefore, WE stand. WE bask in light and love. WE do not judge you or any forms of US. To US there is not right or wrong, no up or down, no hot or cold, only contentment. WE do, however, on all occasions, in your terms, each and every day, send light and love and information to you through time and space, sound, and sight. WE send information to assist you in remembering who you are. This is what WE do. Do you feel US?

WE are your mother's milk, the warm sun upon your face. WE are the rain that falls, the flowers that grow. WE are the tide, the train you caught yesterday. WE are that kiss, that tasty dish of spaghetti. WE are the love you found, WE are the love you lost, and WE are the love you have never known, but will know. WE are the sun, the moon, and the stars. WE are the water that you drink, the food that you eat. WE are the items that you place on your body for covering, which by the way, was never intended to be, yet it is by your choice. WE are the tree, the sail in the wind.

WE are the games that you play and the music that you hear. WE are the cars that you drive and the rocket ships that you use to try to get closer to US. Yet, WE are never far away from you. WE are the dawn and the dew. WE are the short and the tall, the big and the small. WE are the lollipop and the cake. WE are the hat and the coat, the foot and the shoe. WE are simply put, YOU! But WE will continue to tell you who WE are. WE are the photo and the nail. WE are the mountains and the rivers, the valleys and the forest. WE are the never and the ever. WE are the here and the now, the past, and the present. WE are the snow and the mud, the path and the road, the bridge and the stairs. Must WE go on? WE will.

WE are the animal kingdom. WE are over 75,000 species of Phylum Protozoa. WE are the 6,000 species of moss animals and all the Lower Invertebrates. WE are all forms of Amoeba and Ribbon worms. Have not you noticed how the worm churns the soil? Have not you pondered on the sound of the Bush-cricket or the colors of the South African grasshopper? How about the Colorado beetle or the ferocity of the piranha? Please take note of the Mudskippers or the Betta splendens of Thailand, the magnificent fighting fish. How can many of you say WE do not speak to each of you? Maybe you should study up on the lizard with a hump or the Martial eagle, for WE are them and they also are You. Allow US to continue on with this current conversation, as WE ask you about your love affair with the Orangutan and the brotherly love they display when young. Are YOU telling US that you do not feel US when YOU see the Jack rabbit or the Deer mouse? Could it be you do not see US in the Canadian tree porcupine that is a salt addict as many of YOU? Perhaps the Lion or Tiger or Walrus or Elephant do not remain reminders of US? WE, sometimes, gaze in amazement at you as WE watch you watch the Wilson's Storm Petrel dance on the water. Cannot you see US in the beauty of the Pileated Woodpecker or the small Yellow Warbler? Have not some of you taken notice of the Immature Snowy Owl or the great Bald Eagle? It is impossible for the fox and the hound, the dog and the cat, the moose and the fawn not to bring about remembrance of who YOU are. WE are the rat and the chipmunk, the horse and the cow. See US! WE are the fast and the slow, the yes and the no. WE are the maybe and might be. WE are the dance and the song, the lyrics and the melody. WE are the rock and the sand, the bottle and the broom. WE are the mask and the sign, the rum and the wine, the speakers you use and the phone that rings. WE are all things. WE are everything that occurs and does not occur, WE are All which you know and don't know in the World as you know it.

 Most of all, WE do not judge YOU. YOU are US, so too YOU must not allow the misinformation that you were taught or learned in the past from your misinformed teachers to cause you to somehow place a judgment on US. The reason is if you judge US, you will also judge YOURSELF, and this should not be.

 This brings US to the balance of life as you know it. WE will speak to you of life and death, sickness, disease, accidents, and human atrocities as you call them. Calamities such as hurricanes and tornados; these disasters and their occurrences are in their natural states, exactly as your meteorologist and your geologist explain them. When the proper conditions are present and available, they have a high probability of happening. What is important is that YOU must understand that WE are these things also. Then WE will speak to you of your word, "Love."

Hell and Purgatory

However, before WE get to these topics let us inform you about your terms, "Hell" and "Purgatory." They are only a part of US, the WE within your imaginations. Hell and Purgatory were completely formulated within the mind of man. WE will only speak of this once now and remind you later in this manuscript for there is no discussion, except amongst YOURSELVES. THERE ARE NO PLACES KNOWN AS HELL AND PURGATORY. They are totally ridiculous ideas. They were created out of FEAR. What would the purpose of such cells or holding places be and for whom and why? You have been informed that WE do not judge, which also means WE do not Jail. This important question in the minds of many of YOU has been answered. So please, for the sake of YOURSELVES and your home, your planet, your Earth, MOVE ON!

WE MUST INFORM YOU THAT THERE ARE MANY SPIRITS OR SOULS THAT DECIDED NOT TO REMAIN IN THE LIGHT AND LOVE OF THE ONENESS OR STAY IN THEIR CHOSEN REALITY AFTER THE SPLIT. THEY MADE DECISIONS WHICH HAVE CAUSED THEM TO BE RESTRICTED TO A REALM WHICH WE WILL GIVE YOU MORE DETAILED INFORMATION ON LATER.

Lean Not On Your Own Understanding

I finally know why. There are wondrous, superfluous matters. Secrets beyond minimal grasp. Things of birth, life, death. The burrowing of the ant. Cavalcades of celestial bodies impossible to censure. What do I know? Can I explain the Menderes River, its winding course? Percentile of bees to produce honey? After years in Germany, I know nothing of the mystery or magic of the Rune. How is it allowable to percolate so little of the Universe? All a resonance of cause and effect. Perfection not my quality. Epicenters, Godly calls. My concern? I, therefore, digress and defer: yield. I surrender to the MASTER and CREATOR.

II

Life as We Understand It

YOUR life, YOUR manifestation in human form is a choice of YOUR spirit or soul. You are a splinter cell, so to speak, of the All. You are one of the portions or pieces that through free choice chose to experience a different reality than being in the oneness of it All.

You, however, are not included in the bold section mentioned at the conclusion of Chapter I. YOU or Your soul made this agreement to leave the oneness to experience life on your planet as you know it. There are other similar, yet different, portions or pieces of the All that chose the same course as you. They are in or on other planes of existence, on other planets and in other galaxies. A part of your choice and theirs, however, is the consequence of forgetting that you are a part of the oneness. You made a contract (not written on paper) to live a certain number of lives to experience human existence or some other existence, remember who you are, and then return to the oneness. All souls in your category do. Your category is that of being on what you understand to be the Planet Earth. This is how it always was since the time of the great divide, or since your soul made the choice to separate from the Oneness.

A Stumbling Block

This action by your soul and the souls of others brought about a dilemma or problem. Now the problem is (there really are no problems), however, the number of lives one of you lives has increased dramatically in recent times as you know time to be.

Why? Well, the answer is that there has been interference; a stumbling block was created, not by you or the ones of US that remain in the Light. The block has been created by spirits or souls that will be discussed in an upcoming chapter, the ones that are in the realm of existence described in your Christian Bible in the Book of Jude. The description in Verse 6 is partially correct. "And the angels who did not keep their positions of authority but abandoned their own home — these he has kept in darkness, bound with everlasting chains for judgment on the great Day." WE have referenced the [New International Version] for it is easy for most of you to understand.

Some souls, not yours, who did not keep their positions, but abandoned their own home and their subsequent choice after the split from (the Oneness), are kept from obtaining a state of human form or any other physical form on yours or other planets and in other galaxies. They are not kept in chains for any judgment day or everlasting fire. These ones do not experience, what you call, "PEACE" (the profound feeling of well-being of the soul or spirit that flows or comes from the experience of being in synchronization with the ALL, US, or if you like, GOD). They do not feel or experience this because they choose not to. WE will touch upon this later.

Feelings and Emotions You Created

At any rate, your soul wished or desired to create a continued state of creating examples of what you desire to create. They are as follows: Sex, childbirth, and the sensations of touch, sight and sound; also, the emotions or feelings such as joy, anger, apathy, awe, bad, brave, calmness, capableness, cheated, cheerfulness, cleverness, combativeness, confused, destructiveness, determination, disturbed, dividedness, ecstatic, emptiness, enraged, envious, excited, evil, exhausted, fascinated, foolish, frantic, free, glad, goodness, gratified, greedy, grief, guilty, gullible, happy, helpful, helpless, high, homesick, honored, hurt, hysterical, ignored, infatuated, inspired, intimidated, isolated, jealous, kind, lethargic, lazy, lecherous, low, lustful, mad, miserable, mystical, naughty, nutty, obnoxious, obsessed, opposed, outraged, overwhelmed, parsimonious, persecuted, petrified, pleasant, precarious, pressured, pretty, prim, proud, quarrelsome, refreshed, rejected, relieved, remorseful, reverent, righteous, sad, scared, servile, shocked, silly, skeptical, solemn, stingy, stunned, sympathetic, tempted, tenacious, tense, threatened, trapped, ugly, unsettled, left out, violent, vital, wicked, wonderful, worried, zany and fear. These, along with many, many more feelings and emotions, you and your brothers and sisters from other worlds have created. Once again, you are Creators! Informing you of this reality allows you to remember that you cannot blame what you have named "US," "God," or "fate," for what you have in fact, created as your past, present, and future reality. None of the above can be experienced in the All, for WE are together feeling only, what you call, "Pure Love."

Note: Your other brothers and sisters on other planets and such have other names and sound phrases that describe their feelings and, of course, other means of communication that, at this time, would be foreign and impossible for you to understand.

However, WE want you to understand that the radio-frequencies spectroscopy that has revealed water and other organic molecules in interstellar dust clouds should be an indication to you on your home, your planet, your Earth, that there are others similar to you. YOU are not alone!

WE will take time here to briefly speak on the word, "Fear." If there were a possibility of something WE do not like, one example of it would be the feeling or word Fear. Of course, this is not possible, but for your sake WE tell you this feeling or thought is unnecessary and a waste of, what you call, time.

You also need to know and understand that on a larger scale, WE do feel what you do because we are connected. However, it is not how you think. Further this cannot be adequately explained to you at this time. You must reach a higher vibrational level to comprehend what WE mean.

As you go on your way each day, you and all others of your kind are creating what you know or understand as reality. And WE would not have it any other way; for you have total and absolute freedom to do so. Everything, all the things you deem good or bad, happy or sad, are created by you. Notice WE said Everything—You cannot blame US, the All, the WE, for any occurrence; the blame as you call it is all on you. However, because WE are all connected it is also on US. This is what is known to you as a paradox or enigma and will not be understood fully by you until you reach a higher level which many of you are reaching as you read these words. WE are most pleased at the prospect of your coming closer to US, coming closer to your goal of long ago to remember your original self.

Differences Misunderstood

It is time for US to help you remember more — WE shall! The time has come for US to speak to you of what you have named birth defects or deformities, mental illness, and stillbirths. WE must speak to you of this so you may begin to understand that your mind set is not correct in regards to these matters. Many of you when you first chose to take human form or during your possible many opportunities to take human form, decided to enter or re-enter into your world in a state of being that many of you have incorrectly labeled, "deformed."

First WE must tell you that deformed is not a prudent or sound description of these conditions. A more feasible word in your language would be different. The same word should be used for birth defects and mental illness. These ones and many of you in previous lives decided to experience this different form of reality. They or you decided to view your planet from a different perspective, to communicate with others of your kind in a different manner. And, too, are you ready for this one? Give the ones that are different from them the opportunity to reach a higher level of vibration in their past or present reality, by interacting and dealing with them from the position of Light and Love. They give or gave others of your kind the opportunity to reach their higher selves in an accelerated time frame within your time continuum. Now, what do you think of that?

They are souls of a higher vibrational level come to help others be their higher selves. Further, stillborn fetuses decided to give their prospective parents and all concerned the opportunity to learn acceptance in an extemporaneous fashion, the chance to exercise the All in them at a moment's notice and to continue to do so in all matters dealing with every aspect of their human existence the rest of their lives in their present manifestation.

WE shall tell you a true story as it was related to the writer of this book. WE shall recall it to his memory. It happened in your reality, your world. There is in present time a husband and wife who were trying to conceive a child. They tried a number of methods to accomplish such. The child was born with what you have named severe birth defects. The father and mother were in their words, devastated. The mother went into depression and the father cursed US and blamed himself. The father began to use illicit drugs and lost all sense of control. He, after some time, sought help and began to pull it together. He asked doctors and medical professionals why this had occurred to their child. Needless to say, both he and his wife neglected the child. Finally, they were told by a seeker of the light on your planet, your Earth, that to all observers it would appear that the child was beautiful. The child had no one else to depend on for care, comfort, and love, except the mother and father. They were told that the child did not appear to be disabled and that by all outward appearances it was the parents that seemed to be Disabled or unable to function. What do you think?

Now stop for a minute and think of this true story WE just imparted to you. Know from this time forward that All are perfect, everything and everyone, just as it is and appears to be. Therefore, know that in the life and reality that you have created, with quarreling and killing and problems of all sorts, you can change what has arisen in your world — the hate and misunderstanding of your fellowman, the labeling and mistreatment of others. Are you tired of it? Are you tired of discriminations and segregations? What of your dreams and plans being thwarted by yourself or others? Well, you can make a different choice right now. You can change your course, pull up your tent, and stop digging a hole. Right now! You can change your point of view to the real reality.

The Path

My daddy asked me,
"What Path do you Take?"
Before I answered, he said,
"It must be to peace and Grace,
and that would be for the Human Race!"
You see, son, it's all about Grace!
We race around town,
some of us acting like Clowns,
drowning our sorrow in drink,
smoking that weed,
trying not to think!
But, all that takes us away,
away from the real deal!
The deal we all must see!
It's about love and peace!
Those are the things we must reach!
Please, see.
My son, do this for Me!

Continue to read this book; think about what WE are informing you about. Pray about it; ask US for guidance. WE will give it to you. You may rest assured on that. Ask and it shall be given. Seek and you shall find. Knock and the door will be opened. WE have throughout time told you this.

Will you listen this time?

WE tell you to create a new reality for yourself and your world, you can do it! The reason you can do it is you have a choice. You will do it! But will it be in this lifetime? Because now it is time to hit many of you with some unsettling facts.

There is no GOOD or BAD and NO DEATH, not as you perceive them and have been taught to believe!

WE will speak with you in regards to what you consider Good and Bad. These two words are from the mind of man. All is Light and Love; however, there are levels of such. There are different vibrations — some high, some low. (Nothing is good or bad), for whom and what could or would set such parameters, surely, not you or US. Therefore, begin to understand the true nature of All that there is, was, and ever will be.

III

Death

The Autumn of My Life

An epiphany came to me amongst colorful transitory change, during the triangular section of a quadrangular year.

Standing,
as leaves blew around me,
as birds overhead escaped
southward. A feeling of renewal
surrounded me. Peace enfolded
me. Watching squirrels dart
to and fro, as bushy tails hung.
They stored for the winter.
As bears and other creatures
began hibernation.

I was walking into the fall
of my exquisite existence.
Time to prepare for winter.

Eternal Beings

First, understand that no one wants to die! This is implanted within you. You are as is everything in your known universe, eternal, Remember! You are a part of the All that is eternal and everlasting. Therefore, one of the pre-set conditions of your human state is Remembering, if nothing else, that you are an eternal being. Therefore, you don't wish or desire to die as you call it. If, and when, one of your own desires to die or, as you have named it, "commits suicide," something is wrong as you understand wrong to be. The suicidal state or one of giving up on life is an abnormal state of being or not natural. This state of being only occurs when the vibrational level of that person is low and the spirits WE discussed earlier are influencing that individual. Of course, if a higher level of vibration isn't reached, that individual will in fact take his or her own life and possibly that of others.

This is also one of the consequences of being human and on your planet, and of course free choice does come into play. Now, as stated before, "WE do not interfere with free choice." Of course, that individual will have a chance to come back, if he or she chooses to take her or his own life. Coming into human form once again, he or she can correct or make up for that decision if she or he chooses to do so. If he or she chooses otherwise, she or he will have other options. Suicide is not an unforgivable sin as a majority of you have been previously taught by some of your Religionists. All are forgiven. WE will touch upon this later.

Wandering Souls

Our souls wander at night
as we sleep.
They try to find peace.
They mix with other souls
seeking the same.

They dance a private dance.
A dance of harmony and contentment,
a most prolific dance,
a dance in the nothingness of
time and space.

They seek solace from the earthly
constraints of the physical.
They seek that which is contrary to
limited enlisted conditions of
conclusive consciousness.
They seek unity of purpose and thought.
That which, cannot be realized in
an awakened state. They seek each other.

Physical Restrictions and Soul's Contract

WE will continue. Because of the size or magnitude of the soul, if it could be measured, you would be able to see that your human bodies are what you would term hard pressed to contain such. Neale briefly wrote of this in his *Conversations with God* Series. WE implanted within him the analogy of the baby that sleeps for long periods of time. Because of the size of the spirit or soul, the physical containment of that size body is very restrictive and the soul yearns to be free or in a less restrictive area. As one grows older, less sleep is needed, for the soul or spirit is less restricted, although still very restricted. You should also take note of the fact that those individuals that are on a higher level of vibration need less sleep. For when at a very high vibration, the soul desires to remain close to the body to complete as fast as possible the remembrance process in hopes of returning to the oneness faster. Also, individuals that alter their state of being through drugs or some kind of foreign entity also require less sleep for different reasons.

WE will continue. Although your soul chooses to enter into your body on a contract, so to speak, it still aches for freedom from restriction. While you are in human form, working on or trying to remember whom and what you are on a mental level, going about your daily tasks and such, the soul is still waiting, desiring to be with the All. WE explained before that it is an unnatural state to be away from the Oneness and yet still it is by free choice.

Saying all of this, WE are leading to the fact that once your soul is totally separated from its physical form, it is in a state of freedom and in this state has other decisions to consider. Now, however you die as you call it, be it by what you have named natural causes or be it by accident, your soul is free.

This is one of the reasons why, if an individual is in or experiences, what you call, an accident, the soul is released from its physical form during the period of unconsciousness. At this point the soul or spirit has a few decisions to make; i.e.:

- Is it ready to return to US the All?

- Has it completed the task it chose to do in the physical form that it was in?

- Should it return to physical form?

Now, remember freedom of choice is always the major factor. Once the soul or spirit makes that decision, then it follows through with such. Now, of course the condition of the physical body comes into play. Was it damaged or altered? Will the soul come back to your plane of existence in a form as discussed previously in a manner that is designed to help others obtain their higher selves and a higher vibrational level? Many times the soul did in fact contract previously to return in a different manner. What is important for you to understand is that that soul all during this process was in NO PAIN OR DISCOMFORT WHATSOEVER! This fact should help many of you understand the returning of many of your loved ones in a different form as you knew them.

WE are informing you of this, for it is important for many of you to shift your perceptions in regards and reference to your loved ones that may at this current time be in hospitals or other types of care facilities. Their appearance or behaviors may be different from the way they were before. Remember, their souls are in no pain.

ABORTIONS

This brings us to what you have named "abortions," a subject that many of you deem necessary to hurt or kill one of your others over. Let us first ask any of you that may feel so passionate (being passionate over something is, as you say, okay) over this or any subject, if you feel it is in the highest good to harm another over your so-called beliefs or passions? WE tell you this:

It is not of a high vibration to do so. Say what you will, it is not. Further WE have explained that all souls have contracts, therefore, even the ones that you feel are aborted by someone do, too. It is not just the choice of the parents or parent or some concerned person, it is also the choice of the child. Yes, WE said child. For at the moment of conception, one of you is, what you call, "human." It is from this point on that freedom of choice comes into play. And of course WE would have it no other way.

WE have also informed you that no one can judge, for, you know not what you are judging. If you do remember who and what you are, US, then most certainly you would be working on raising your own vibrational level, setting a high example or standard for others. This, of course, would include the highest choice of not hurting your sacred self or others for their choices. It is the universe that, by the choice of the one that you say or claim has been aborted, will send that one back into total Light and Love, or into some other form of manifestation.

The preceding statements may anger many of you, so be it. WE tell the absolute truth. After the truth, the course of action is of course your choice. However, in the moment or moments of anger, will those of you who are angered act at a high level of vibration or not? WE will watch, WE will wait, WE will see. Whatever any of you do, WE will not judge!

Remember,

We Love You.

Letting Go or Releasing

Also, Neale wrote in his books of how many of you, through your worry and misunderstandings, hold or interfere with many souls that are in a ready state to leave your plane of existence to depart from their bodies. Through your combined vibrational levels, you and your concerned loved ones can cause and draw a soul back to your plane when they are actually ready to move on.

This is a matter many of you should ponder over. Many of you will obtain a level of freedom and peace not known to you before by letting go of those souls and allowing them to continue on their chosen path. From US informing you of this, you should be able to understand and remember more about collective consciousness and its power on a larger scale. Power, that can and will effect change within your societies, your world, and your Earth as you know it, if you just allow it.

Death Misunderstood

Your outlook on death should thus also be adjusted in regards to how each of you view both manmade and natural disasters that are a part of it All. It is important for you to know that the thousands that, as you call it, "die or perish" during such occurrences or anomalies that may be classified as calamities, such as tsunamis, earthquakes, and the like, do not suffer. It may appear to the human eye that they do. They appear as you understand it to be, crying out in pain and suffering.

However, what you witness is only those portions of their being, the physical and mental, which as WE explained before does not wish to die. It is the human mind at this point that processes the misinformation previously received from whatever source or sources taught them or instilled in them the preconceived meanings or concepts of what separation from the physical or the word death is like.

Thus, these beings recall and bring forth from deep within their analytical or logical minds the accumulation of all subconsciously retained or acquired information concerning their understanding of death. Yes, every bit given to them within their time frame in physical form comes rushing forth. This causes the human being to react in a fashion that translates or appears to translate into fear.

This fear, which WE have already touched upon, is unnecessary, for any of you perceiving that your being would be in any other state other than Love and Light is the problem. So as it appears to human sight, these persons are suffering when they are not. They are fighting what they think and perceive will happen to them if they die, which is once again, in the mind of man, "dying."

Ending this discussion WE once again reemphasize that they are not suffering, only reacting. For when they are as you call it, "dead," in an instance they realize peace, calm, and joy beyond your current understanding. Therefore, you see, death is not as it appears to be.

Contacts From the Otherside

Adding to this, your loved ones can't and don't come back in the spirit form to talk to you. For what reason would this be? You do not need their help. You have Angels and other assistance. Again, your relatives will either return in a new manifestation of the physical within your current realm of existence or in another. If this is not the case, they will return to the light and love that is All that there is, from whence they came.

Therefore, spirit mediums that claim to be channeling your relatives that have passed over are, in fact, most times duping or deceiving you and themselves. Now they may be channeling some kind of spirit or entity, but they are not your loved ones. Most times these persons receive a piece or fragment of small remnants of your loved ones' memory floating or remaining within the cosmos. These remnants are thus received by a guardian angel or some other entity in non-physical form and then transferred to you through a medium. However, once again, it is not your loved one as you understand them to be or to have been.

With this being said, you should know that many of the self-proclaimed mediums use or play on the grief and pain of others to obtain monetary gain or profit. Most of these are, in fact, under the influences of lower vibrational spirits that cause them to believe they are communicating with the dead. These are not to be trusted or sought out for advice and comfort. Remember, there is no right or wrong, yet most of these mediums are not coming from a space of high vibration and, once again, are under the direct influence of the spirits that WE have informed you of. WE will discuss this later within this book of information.

Many of you will be upset by this information WE are giving you now. However, WE give you the plain truth. Accept it or not, it is of course your choice and it will affect your future someway, somehow. There are, WE must say, many well-intended persons that receive messages from guardian angels and have misinterpreted it to believe that they are in direct communication with the dead. WE hope this information raises their vibrational level to the point of understanding that they will and can help many on your home, your planet, your Earth, if they readjust their thinking, accept this information, and remember who they really are. They are gifted persons in contact with angels who are giving them fragmented information to help others live in the here and now.

How will you know who these ones are? Of course, WE will tell you. For, WE wish and desire for all to obtain and maintain high levels of vibrations. You will know those that are sincere by this: They will speak of light and love. They will inform all that the information they are receiving is for the concerned person or persons still in physical form to receive, discern, and move on with their lives. And the proof will be in the pudding, so to speak. The persons that are given help (information) will move past any attachment with obsessions of contacting their "passed over," as you call it, loved ones again. They will proceed on with their own lives. All on Planet Earth should let go of all unnecessary attachments with the dead as you understand the dead to be. It is important for you to know that holding on to yesterday's memories causes unfulfilled todays and tomorrows.

IV

The Physical Body

What's Good, What's Not

Tis, Tis, Tis!

How did I end up here?
In a dark frame of mind.
Living in fear, smoking and drinking beer!

My life a wreck, my mind a mess,
Dizzy, distorted, confused.

Where can I go? What can I do?

If I continue to live like this,
A life without bliss, no joy,
no love, no fun.

Alone.
Painful days, sleepless nights.
I just can't continue to live like this!

Sickness, Infections, and Disease

All is perfect as is. However, a consequence of being in your now current human form is becoming ill or sick. For OUR purposes of explaining this human feature WE will use this definition of Sickness, "being in a state other than Oneness." This means that since you have chosen to take a physical form and be apart from US, you became susceptible, open, and vulnerable to disorders and diseases. Therefore, this leads to the possibilities of declines, weaknesses, fevers, frailties, infections, and general states of poor health. WE, in the stillness of the All, are in total order as you once were. Therefore, WE being within order cannot be within disorder or disease and, therefore, no state of decline or weakness which, in turn, leads to no possibility of the other mentioned symptoms that you experience in physical form. You must take in breath as you have named it to live or function.

This opens you to infections which are impurities transferred or transmitted into your digestive, respiratory, or circulatory systems. These germs are microorganisms that end up where they are not supposed to be. Now since all is connected and really not apart, another paradox, most if not all objects on your planet, inanimate and animate, are made up of the same basic elements with different variations. This, if you follow logical thought patterns, makes them a piece of you, only in different forms that should be in a different space or not in you in more than the trace minute amounts needed for your particular manifestation.

A good example would be how your kind may contract Lyme disease, which involves a spirochete bacterium transmitted to you by ticks. Humans are not the preferred hosts for this disease. For these ticks, the bacterium are most often sustained on deer and mouse populations. Your human movements sometimes interfere with these populations, which in turn interfere with the ticks, thus causing potential exposure to you and the disease. So, you should be able to see how the total ecology which is together, yet apart, can intermix, thus causing various human dilemmas.

Let's also take a look at the Ebola virus. Your planet's investigators know that these viruses are a section of exotic viral agents that cause severe hemorrhagic fever disease in humans and in some other primates. They make up a group of pathogenic agents known as Filoviridae. They appear as long thin rods. They are made up of a single species of ribonucleic acid molecule that is bound together with special viral proteins and is surrounded by a membrane coming from the outer membrane of infected cells. WE are making an attempt to explain it in a simple manner for you. Now, when buds from the surface of these cells are released, pointed portions that are on the surface recognize and attach to specific receptor molecules on the surface of a susceptible cell and in turn penetrate the cell. Added to your human problem is the fact that very little is known of the ecology of Ebola and the natural hosts of filoviruses remain unknown to you at this present time. However, many of you are working on it and will come up with more answers soon.

But here is the point; this virus is spread primarily through contact with an infected individual, his or her body fluids, or some other source of infectious material. Rapid deterioration of an individual begins as the integrity of the circulatory system becomes affected. All of the contacts in each step are a natural part of your world, your planet, your home.

Any sickness or ailment of the human being is a direct effect of your being outside the oneness. Yet, there is hope. Once you begin to obtain a higher level of vibration, you can train your body to reject and dispose of the diseases, germs, and any disorder that has entered into a particular place or space in your being where they are not supposed to be.

Tools to Health

Also you can realign areas of your being such as the spine, knees, and other parts to regain youth and agility. You and your kind can replace much needed missing or depleted vitamins and minerals through treatments using essential oils and other homeopathic medications. You can raise the vibrational level of your bodies with the biofeedback consciousness, thus returning to healing oneself as you did before on your home, your planet, your Earth. It would be a good idea for you to look into the biofeedback method of healing — you will be surprised.

Touch therapy, too, and many more methods and modalities are available to mankind. And WE will of course help you. WE have given or sent much information to humankind just within what you term as the last three years. And there are people on your home, your planet, your Earth, to assist you. All you need do is ask. There are those whom can and will teach you of Reiki, Quantum Touch healing, and the use of sound vibrations with crystal bowls to bring your energy fields in line with the universe. Classes and seminars on meditation and intuitive thinking will become more available to you. Contemplating universal answers to your personal questions will be made easier by walking labyrinths and simple coloring of Mandelas, "a tool given to humankind from the universe designed in terms of sacred geometry, used to connect one's physical being to US."

Many other avenues to higher levels of consciousness will become more apparent to all of you. More of you will seek out methods and modalities to uplift your spirit. WE, of course, set this into motion with your assistance. All of you are ready for a change for yourself and your world. Is not this a wonderful prospect? WE may point to the recent election in America; man and womankind in general are becoming ready to as you call it, "grow up," and WE would have it no other way.

It is time to speak out about what happened to you, all of you. There has occurred over millions of, what you call, "years," a great shift in the polarities of your being. Why? WE will, you may rest assured, tell you.

The Slowing Brain

Your body, primarily your brain and nerves, have electric currents, although they do not work in the same fashion as a wire leading to your computer. Now, as you understand it, electricity is the movement of a charge. In an electrical cord or wire the electrons move to carry a charge though the wire. Within the nerves in your body the electrical signal moves; however, there is no electrical charge. Now, the insides of nerve cells contain a slight negative charge as a result of the flow which moves ions predominantly out of a cell. When a charge is forced to a nerve cell, it causes gates or doors in a membrane to open. In turn, this causes the ions to reenter the cell and depolarizes the membrane, thus closing to the position where the charge originated from. This depolarization causes ion channels to open in a membrane down the line within the nerve. This causes another depolarization which opens up channels in the membrane to bring about a chain reaction of depolarizations until it reaches the end, where responses occur such as the movement of a finger or toe.

Now, what are WE telling you? WE are telling you that over the course of time as you know it, the human brain, which is the origin of most electrical stimulation within your body, has slowed down dramatically during the process of transferring certain currents into electrical reactions. As briefly described above, your brain does not react as fast as it once did; thus, causing and bringing about the end result of your body's being out of synchronization with the universe.

Therefore, all of your functions, everything you do has become slower than it was meant to be. It is important for all of humankind to understand that the computer that your kind utilizes is only a replica of your brain. Therefore, guess what? Your brain should and can work just as fast as any computer. This ability on all levels of thinking and reaction is possible now, just as it was in a time gone by. Many of you do understand this and it is time for all of you to clearly remember and understand this once again.

Currently on your planet, your brain uses only approximately 8.76% of its capacity. You have been socially, environmentally, and culturally lobotomized. It is therefore wishful thinking at the best to say as most of your learned researchers claim you use ten percent.

If you find this hard to digest just do some research on Neurology studies and other documented studies on MRIs and brain scans. As WE insist all throughout this book, research for yourself; you are able to do so. Do not believe, as all of you have done so eagerly in the past, everything you are told by others. It is OUR purpose and intent to assist you in obtaining higher personal and global awareness. This brings you closer to US, closer to whom and what you really are.

WE fully understand that many on your home, your planet, your Earth are concluding and will try to find ways to disprove what WE are giving you within this book. Good, as you understand the word good to be. WE would have it no other way. You see, the more you question, the more true answers come to you. Is not this a clever saying? WE, that which includes you, came up with it. And if you seek; yes, it is true, you will find.

The Process

The qualitative and analytical
processes of my mind
A mystery to me.
Before I make that mistake,
do I hesitate?
Do I determine the
subjective proportions of
outcomes and consequences of
belated actions, transferred
from the cornerstone of the
cortex, the cerebral, and
cerebellum-wet hemispheres
of my being?
Or are my thoughts dorsal
ornaments hanging in darkness?
I put forth this question to self.
If reasonable man I be, why not
total sound judgment and piercing
goodness spring from me?
Instead, wishy-washy man I be!

Let US also look at the human eye. This magnificent portion of your being is so intricate that the most sophisticated telescopes and cameras are, as well as the copiers, just poor replicas. In your natural state, there would be no use for glasses or what you have named "contact lenses." There is no reason for any of you to need or use these items and WE have given you such technology to cease these practices. Therefore, it would be, as you call it, a good idea to look into the remedies available to you such as laser surgeries on your home, your planet, your Earth.

Concluding this section, WE tell you also that human reflex was faster at one time. Your bodies were able to heal much faster, and of course you were able to do any and every task you could think of much faster. You were able to accomplish feats you only dream of now but which you can accomplish once again, if only you remember who you are!

Notice how speed records are being broken so frequently now. Why or how do you think this is so? WE will tell you, you as humans are using the training and technology WE gave you to enhance your physical being. Please note WE are not speaking of hormone-changing drugs. Anything not natural is, shall WE say, not good for you, as you understand good to be.

All of this, the slowing down, the lack of the ability to remember things, and the way you care for your home Earth and yourself is a direct result of being apart from US, as well as the experimentations you and your kind have done with what you place in and on your bodies. Now as always, you have a choice. WE will impart the correct information to you. What you do with it is up to you.

WE LOVE YOU!

Fasting and Purging

Many of the sicknesses and illnesses that your kind experience are due to the fact that you place unnecessary items or substances into or on your being. WE have explained before that there are many chemicals and minerals which your being should only have trace amounts of. WE wish to assist you in enabling your bodies and minds to move towards how you once were. The following things can help you.

Your bodies should be purged periodically. Fasting should be accomplished on a limited basis, once or twice a year will suffice. Anything more than this could be dangerous to your being. When fasting is planned, it should be for no longer than a three-day period. When one undertakes this purge, it should be for the purpose of cleansing the body of unneeded and unnecessary toxins only. WE shall inform you that you have no need to fast to get closer to US; WE are always with you, in you, under you, over you, totally around you. This information should also separate many of you from fanatical groups and individuals that do not have your best interests or unbeknownst to them, theirs, at heart.

Now, the reason you should not fast for more than a three-day period is as follows. First, this is all the time you need. Within this time frame, if you drink water and intake small portions of raw vegetables, your digestive system will adjust and remove the necessary particles that need to be removed. Your blood, your life force, will be cleansed.

Further, if you partake in this practice any longer than suggested, any of your medical doctors should be able to verify for you the following: Within less than one day, the basic energy requirements of your being will begin to falter. Glucose and glycogen are stored in only small amounts. However, the quantities of triacylglycerols can and will provide the necessary energy requirements. You can, for up to seventy days and over a year in the case of obese persons, maintain these basic energy requirements with triacylglycerols stored in your fat cells. But why would you wish to do that? And if body protein is available one could fast longer, but WE tell you once again this is unnecessary and unneeded.

The human glycogen in the liver will fall to about nine percent of its needed concentration and stay within this limit for the period needed to purge. Your muscle glycogen will decrease. Your blood glucose level will remain acceptable. However, once the amount of metabolized glycogen begins to become exhausted, the rate of triacylglycerols, used in the fat depots of the abdominal and subcutaneous areas, will increase. Triacylglycerol oxidation will bring about the rising of blood ketone levels and a fall or reduction in respiratory functions. Within the second or third day, the amounts of nitrogen excreted in the urine will increase. Amino acid catabolism will start and the body proteins will degrade. Therefore, those biological functions that depend upon protein as fuel will become impaired. Now because your brain has a high metabolic rate, it normally uses only glucose as fuel. During a fast when the glucose level falls, many disturbances in the functions of your central nervous system will occur. Now, since the liver glycogen is almost depleted after the first day of fasting, blood glucose must be manufactured from other sources to meet the needs of your brain. Therefore, it would be a good idea or decision for those of you who feel it is important for you to fast any longer that you should do some serious investigation.

The bottom line is that your body will make for you a series of calculated choices to utilize the body protein during fasting to keep the central nervous system functional. However, only three days of this is all that is needed. Now WE tell you this, because WE LOVE YOU, and because you need all of your being to be functional at all periods of time. There is much for each of you to complete in the course of one of your days. Therefore, LOVE YOURSELF, and do not place unneeded stress on your bodies!

Food, Products, and Negative Use of Time

Now is the time to speak to you of the foods you eat. WE will only speak to you briefly of this for it is simple.

Anything on your home, your Earth, your planet, that is digestible, with the exception of poisonous or harmful food items to your being, may be consumed for human intake. It is important for you to remember this fact. There are those of you who judge others for what they eat. And, of course, this is not of a high vibration.

Over the course of your human history, WE have placed within the mind of man what is edible and through trial and error you have helped yourselves find those things which are not. WE LOVE YOU and do not wish for you to incur the unnecessary self-defeating mind games you place on yourselves sometimes. However, WE will say this. Read, investigate, and discern for yourselves what products in your stores are unnecessary or unneeded, the preservatives and such that may be used. Remember, you have freedom of choice, OUR greatest gifts to YOU, for YOU are US and WE are YOU, and none of YOU are FOOLS despite what YOU may have been trained or told to believe!

The eating of animals is okay! WE tell you this; animals are placed in and have chosen their relative positions on your Earth for their purposes. And those that are edible, consumable, and digestible have no problem with the food chain or being consumed by you, and neither should you have issues with doing so. It is the circle of, what you call, life. And they also (please understand this) have free choice. Do not, for one moment, assume they haven't. Your hunters and fishermen innately understand this. They understand well the days they get many and the days they get none. They got none, for it was not the day. Farming animals such as cattle, other livestock, farmed fish, and all other animals within these categories are fair game and were created by you for your convenience. Furthermore WE placed this, shall WE say, within the mind of man. Do you really think you came up with this on your own? And WE have no say on these issues; WE do not dwell in your realm, except through you, so, therefore, WE do assist you.

The wearing of Furs and usages of wool and other material derived from animal skins and hides, as well as many other customs regarding what you place on your bodies, on your planet, are okay. There will, of course, be many who disagree with this on your home, your planet, your Earth. That would be their decision. They have free choice; WE will however tell them that time spent on elevation of one's being is the best course for all. And ask them this question: Is their time spent worrying and planning to stop others from enjoying the bounties of your wonderful Earth time well spent on the elevation of their being?

WE would add that, there are many activities on your home, your planet, your Earth, such as protesting over excessively, too much masturbation, and hours, upon hours, on the Internet (of course there is nothing wrong with spending a reasonable time on the net for entertainment, researching items, or shopping) which could be put to a better use. All of you understand what a reasonable length of time is to devote to the above-mentioned activities. WE don't have to tell you. Furthermore, sarcasm, and the killing of animals for any other reasons other than for food, clothing, or self-defense are also all unnecessary practices and a waste of, what you call, "time."

More examples would be building an unneeded over supply of condominiums or houses (note now the lack of the ability to acquire a home or credit that you have created on your planet) and other time-consuming activities not used to improve one's vibrational level; these are all, as are many other things on your planet, distractions. These are distractions from loving, living, giving, laughing, and remembering who and what you are. Further, many of these bring about greed which is the root to your planet's current ongoing financial crisis. WE tell all of you, if you would spend more time working on raising your personal vibration, you would not have to bail-out anyone or anything. Don't believe US — take a good look around you and think about it. It will come to you. WE love you!

As for the products you use on your bodies, such as shampoos, lotions, and the like, the same rule applies, read the labels. There are many natural consumer products. It would be wise and a loving decision on your part to use the items that are best for your total being. Of course WE could give you a list of all that you should use, but what fun would that be! WE would be doing the work for you. You would not be creating which is your natural self. Just create yourself anew, A New Way of looking at what you use on your precious bodies. You can do it, WE believe in you!

WE hope the next series of statements gives many of you relief. Understand that the following statements are true:

> The Earth, as you know it, will stand until the end of time as you know it, which by the way is FOREVER! However, if you and your kind do not begin to function on a higher vibrational level in mass and as a more cohesive group, many of you will perish, as many cultures and whole civilizations have in past human history. And this will be as it always was, just as represented by the name of one of your popular television shows, *Without A Trace*.

> Know this: Disappearances of whole societies as you understand societies to be has happened before and will once again, unless dealt with. It is no mystery; the ones who did not take care of themselves as individuals, or collectively care for the elderly, were certainly not seeking higher levels of vibration. Therefore, any of you who are intolerant of any of your kind is a FOOL! For, it is written I AM, YOU ARE, WE ARE, ONE! Any deviation from this is a LIE!

ARE YOU LIVING A LIE?

IT IS OF COURSE YOUR CHOICE!

V

Love of Self and Others: Relationships

You Ask Me When I Knew

Of course I did not want to answer this. I thought you might find me amiss, if you knew the cold hard facts. You would think me a simpleton within my mind. For where I come from, one must not admit he fell in love upon the first touch of lips. Let me be forth-with; it was even before the kiss when I first laid eyes upon your face. To my mind came, "God, thank you for this grace, this mercy you place upon me, to send an angel from above, to send me love at first sight." I prayed with all my might this be real, the way I feel. Then once I heard your voice, I simply had no choice. The course was laid, the road already paved.

There Is A Place

There is a place where your
heart can be,
A place where bluebirds fly
and your eyes will never cry.
A place of the moonlit kiss,
and hot steamy morning bliss.
A place of no rejection, only
tender love and sweet affection.
A place where love is no game,
A place where love can't be tamed.
A place where love dances and has
all its wonderful chances.
A place where the sky is beaming,
love has real text, real meaning.
Would not you like to see
this place where love runs free?
This place reserved for you and me?
Why don't you come along and see!
This place where your heart can be!

Love

What shall WE say of love? Love is to comprehend, understanding YOU are all there is, so act accordingly.

Practice Self-Love

Treat yourself and pamper yourself. Buy nice clothes. Dress to impress YOU. Wear what you want as long as you harm not yourself or others in doing so. Each of you absolutely understands the times you live in; you know what is good for you and what is not. WE don't have to tell you this, nor does anyone else. Search within yourself. Ask yourself a series of questions each day. Lean towards your mirror and say:

- Am I clean?

- Will I offend anyone by too little or too much fragrance? What kind of fragrances do I use?

- Does what I have on cause me to feel that I AM WONDERFUL, that I AM LOVE?

Now please, do the aforementioned with the rings you put on, the watches, the shoes, and so forth and so on.

If you won't do it for yourself, who else will? Further, ask yourself, are the products I am putting on my skin a reflection of I AM WONDERFUL, I AM LOVE?

- Are they good for my skin, are they abrasive?

- Do they cause me to feel good, are they needed?

- At the conclusion of your day ask: Have I done all I can to interact peacefully with others this day?

Respect and Care of Possessions

Love and care for everything within your home or place of dwelling whatever or wherever it may be. It could be a house or an apartment. It could be a trailer home or cardboard box. It does not matter! Clean it, care for it, look at it, and ask yourself, "Does this place, this home of mine say I AM WONDERFUL, I AM LOVE?" If not, do something to change it. You CAN!

And the same thing holds true of all you possess, ANYTHING! If it does not reflect YOU ARE LOVE and LIGHT, move away from it, change it, and dispose of it, if necessary. Replace it. Empower yourself. You CAN!

WE tell you this, YOU DESERVE THE BEST. Please, OUR Dear Ones, understand and adhere to this, subscribe to it. It is the beginning of remembering Who YOU Are.

The Best Foods

Eat the best foods for you. You know what they are. Eat that cake, if you desire. Yet, know thee this. The whole cake may not be best for you. Eat candy, why not? It would, however, not be best for you to eat the whole box in one sitting. You know this. WE are only reinforcing what you already know, to help you remember. Go to the health food store. Buy organic products and the other as well, as long as they are good for you as you understand good to be.

Family

Love your family, the direct ones as you understand the bloodline, be it your grandparents, your mother, father, sisters, or brothers. If you do not know your direct bloodline, love your family as you know it to be. Is what you are doing best for you and for them? Come on, you know the answer. It is not that hard. Treat them with respect and honor. If you have wronged them, or they think you have wronged them, apologize to them. It is written, "Pride before the crash." Visit them, invite them over, talk with them in person or, if you cannot do so, use your phone. Send gifts and cards. Hug them, believe US, it is contagious and infectious; you will be surprised at what occurs. Encourage them, empower them, thus empowering yourself. However, do not enable them by their negative selves to remain at a low vibrational level. Assist them in reaching higher, to the stars, to US.

May These Things Be!

MAY YOUR LIFE BE FILLED WITH MIRTH AND CHEER!
MAY YOUR HEART BE FULL OF JOY AND LAUGHTER!
MAY YOUR HOME HAVE LOVE AND FAMILY CHATTER!
MAY YOUR SOUL BE FULL OF PEACE!
MAY ALL YOUR DREAMS COME TRUE!
MAY FAMILY AND FRIENDS REMAIN CLOSE TO YOU!
MAY ALL THESE THINGS BE FOR YOU!

Platonic Love

Treat the friends you have as you treat yourself. Encourage them to be their best, reinforce to them that they are the creators of their own destiny. Spend time with them, support them in their endeavors. Spread the word to them of your planet's coming of age in regards to a higher vibration; yes, inform all of your friends of the remembering process. Be a light in the dark for them and for yourselves.

Also, as with your biological family, ask yourself the same questions in your day by day dealings with them. Visit them, invite them over, and talk with them. Send cards and letters. Hug them, believe in them. Encourage them. Empower them, thus empowering yourself. However, do not enable them in any attempts by the negative self to stammer or stagger themselves from reaching the highest vibrational level possible.

Romantic Love

This of course brings US to Romantic Love — that idea, that feeling each of you aspires to reach, to feel. Guess what? This idea or thought is implanted within you. It is the lasting remnant or reminder of your being in oneness, in ecstasy, in pure joy and contentment. For know this, it is not within the mind of man and woman to be alone. You were not made as such nor were any of the creators like you in other places or other times. WE did place within the mind of OUR son, Neale Donald Walsch, a magnificent explanation of such, of the chemistry between man and woman. It would behoove you to read it.

Nevertheless, here WE shall take it further for you are ready. You are the creator of yourself and your reality. The preceding is a fact. There is no debating. You may wish to do so; however, the point is mute and a waste of time. And, of course, it is your choice. Once again, you create.

WE are Love. YOU are Love. YOU are US, WE are YOU. WE, US, YOU are apart yet together. When YOU were displaced from US, certain causes and effects occurred. One of these is the innate ability of your desire to be one. Now, it is impossible to be one physically or sexually with all on your planet at the same time. Now, you could be one with all, one person at a time, however, you would cause certain demise of self in the attempt to do so. Therefore, the ability to intertwine or become joined or joint with another of your kind was provided by US and by YOU. This is the reason the human body is designed as it is for sexual intercourse and reproductive purposes.

Biology and Love 101

Let us examine this. This is important for each of you to fully understand. It is for you. WE do not live or dwell within your realm. With that said, WE move on. Some of you know and remember much of this, many don't. The human male's sexual organs are located inside and outside the pelvis. The male genitals include the duct system (epididymis and vas deferens), the accessory glands which house the seminal vesicles and prostate gland, and the penis along with the testicles. The penis rids the body of urine or liquid waste and serves as the instrument for ejaculation of sperm.

The human female's organs are contained within the pelvis. The external part of the female reproductive organ is the vulva, which means covering. Located between the legs, the vulva covers the opening to the vagina and other reproductive organs located inside the body. The fleshy area located just above the top of the vaginal opening is called the mons pubis. The skin flaps or labia surround the vaginal opening. The clitoris, a small sensory organ, is located toward the front of the vulva where the folds of the labia join. Between the labia are openings to the urethra, which is the canal that carries urine from the bladder to the outside of the body, and the vagina. The female vagina has three purposes: the place or port for the penis during intercourse, the pathway that babies travel through or birth canal, and the route for menstrual blood to exit the body from the uterus.

Why do WE discuss this? Misinformation has plagued humankind throughout your history. WE wish to set the record straight. This is the manner and nature of sexual intercourse. You may of course practice different variations. You have freedom of choice. And of course, WE do not judge or care what you do; WE simply love you. However, WE tell you this, that the above-mentioned are the only extensions or orifices designed for the human sexual experience by the US, the YOU, the WE. All other sexual experiences and positions are from the mind of humankind, and that's permitted also. This is another paradox: There are personal consequences in your present manifestations for stepping outside the natural order of things that must be dealt with mentally and physically. It is of course up to you! WE would have it no other way.

Homosexuality

This brings US to Homosexuality. WE do not judge. WE impart to you the facts and WE love you no matter what you do. You may deviate as you wish; you may experiment all you desire. Yet, whatever you may decide to do in reference to the idea that you call love, do it with love of self and others in mind. For, it is important that all of you remember: Love has no bounds; love is not restrictive. It cares not of gender; it cares not of ethnic situation, it cares not of age. Love cares only for self. Love cares to be given and not as much to be received. Love does not discriminate. Whomsoever you love, send cards and letters, hug them, and believe in them. Encourage them, empower them; thus, empowering yourself. However, do not enable them in any attempts by the negative self to stammer or stagger themselves from reaching the highest vibrational level possible.

Gay Marriages

Yes, encourage all you have contact with or may come in contact with that the time is now to raise their vibrational level. It is you who set your laws governing love and marriage. It is also you who change them just as the wind shifts directions as it decides to do so. Each of you may have romantic relationships with whom you desire. Now, here's the question to ask of self: Is this really what I understand and know love to be? If it is, proceed as long as your love harms not yourself or the other or others. No one can judge you; if one does, one is, indeed, judging oneself.

The Hermaphrodite

Of the hermaphrodite. It is time to address what many of you do not understand nor will understand or embrace if you are currently at a low level of vibration — those born as you term it, "without prior sex assigned gender or born with both genitalia (penis and vagina)."

They or anyone who came to your known world this way was, of course, sent or returned by self to help others be their highest selves. They have, as each and every one of you do, the male and the female internally; the difference is that they also have both externally. There are many other species on your home, your planet, your Earth with this dual sexual design

(Clownfish, Banana Slugs, snails and earth worms), all what you would consider "able to self-fertilize." You do not judge or shun them, do you? You do not scientifically reject or call them freaks of nature, do you? Well, possibly those amongst you who remain uneducated or on a low vibrational level, may adversely label these portions of your universe.

WE point out here that those of you who could not (or would not) accept the hermaphrodite just as they are — different — will later, or did previously, return to a human physical form repeatedly until they fully understood and remembered that all are the same. This fact also goes for all who refuse to accept any race, human being, or manifestation different from themselves. Now, also this includes any manifestation that made repeated decisions during this lifetime or other lifetimes to harm, kill, or continually mistreat others different from them. You must accept all, for all are you. This is known as the (law of acceptance) in the known universe. It was set into place by US, by YOU.

Whenever one of your kind or any other of your brothers or sisters in any realm of existence refuses to accept any certain situation or situations, or others like you (for all are like you, only some are different), it causes a lowering of that one's vibrational level which opens that one up to all sorts of harmful and hurtful things, not to mention another unnecessary lifetime somewhere within the time continuum.

Remember, Remember!

Child Abuse

WE will at this point sincerely ask those who choose to practice any forms of child abuse, child pornography, or engaging in sex with children: What are you thinking? Does this belief or practice in any way, shape, form, or fashion suggest a high level of vibration? Does it lead to a clear uncluttered path to whom and what you really are?

WE will not ever tell you what to do or punish you. WE have, however, placed within the human mind the appropriate ages for the sexual experience to begin. And of course, it is not under the age of (14) fourteen. The human body and mind were not made to withstand the physical and emotional trauma that occurs when the sexual intercourse process begins under that age. Many cultures have and do deviate from this universal fact and do, in fact, create the circumstances related to such.

Each of you understands fully what cultures you live in and the laws that govern such. All of you understand age limitations for the locations where you live on your home, your planet, your Earth. It would, therefore, be in your highest interest to follow such and not cause yourself or others undo and unnecessary hardships. It is, of course, up to you, you do have absolute freedom of choice and you will absolutely reap the consequences of your actions from the sons of men and women. WE did not say consequences from US. WE do not live in the physical; you do. Of course, your species does not take these actions lightly. WE shall further inform you that in the realm you live in, you reap what you sow! You have created such, not US.

The Male and Female — Equality

Of male and female. While WE are at this point, WE must inform you that contrary to some beliefs there are no measurable or outstanding deviations between males and females as a whole, unless such deviations are set within the DNA at the moment of, what you call, "conception." These differentiations begin immediately as your humankind develops within the womb with little exception. There are some minor differences in the general structure of the male and female brains. However, WE tell you they are only due to factors such as hormones and other materials within your being and they really, hear US, don't make a difference. Neither Males nor Females are superior in any area. However, there are those on higher vibrational levels within both genders. When all is said and done, ALL ARE EQUAL!

There are both men and women on your home, your planet, your Earth, that share equal responsibility for the conditions of your world. There are both men and women who go unrecognized for what they do, caring for their families and communities. In all countries, there is still discrimination of the sexes. Poor people are denied education and medical care. Both men and women play a part in this. Both men and women are capable of violence and, what you call, "adultery." Both men and women fight over land and religions. Both men and women are Christians and Muslims. Both men and women suffer from psychological torments. Both men and women can be and many are, as you have named them, "cops" and "robbers." Both men and women carry bombs to kill themselves and others. Both men and women cheat and lie in the name of God and country. Poverty and disease impact men and women, moms and dads, boys and girls. Both men and women make lots of money and there are both men and women who can barely make ends meet. Many are in dire straits and suffer. Both men and women are imprisoned and under the spells of addictions. Both men and women fight in wars and both heal the sick. Both men and women attend colleges and universities. Both men and women vote and run for public offices. Now is there total equality for both? No! But it is not OUR doing, it is yours.

Yes, now as it stands and appears in the sands of time, men have caused themselves to have a somewhat advantage. But WE tell you this; there was a time when women had the advantage and acted as men do now. If you carefully research, you will find documents and supporting information that touch upon the ideas of matriarchal societies. Many sociologists and anthropologists point to prehistoric evidence of such. Ancient writings lead to what many of you call "theories." WE, however, tell you they are not just theories. If you look, WE mean, put the modern family under the microscope and examine the family in its entirety, you will see a pattern of men protecting women. Men always have had this role, they were sent out by women to guard the villages and do the hard labor, as they are also today.

It was only after the male species began to think he could rule better than his counterpart, that the current mind set prevalent today took hold. The new leaders, as you call them, "men" foolishly self-proclaimed themselves the head of the household. Then he ventured out and brought war and instability back to their villages, which now in turn covers your home, your planet, your Earth. Men have always and will always, protect and follow those you understand to be the "female."

It has only been in what you have come to know as modern history that women have been called "second-class baby factories." Women were the leaders of the original ancient tribes and are still today in portions of your world (China, South India, and some Caribbean tribes) just to name a few. And, if you really remember, you will see clearly that on your home, your planet, your Earth, they still are the leaders. Do not be mislead, "Vanity, vanity, all is vanity. Nothing is new under the sun." You can rest assured this is true.

Note of Caution

A cautionary note must be added here; there are those whom will make attempts to use the above-mentioned statements to justify the rationale that there is one gender, as you understand genders, that should rule or be in leadership positions. WE, however, inform you that the roles of leadership should be equally homogenized between men and women. This, of course, would be the scenario for the highest good of all. WE will speak more on the subject of power later within this text.

Remember!

What Will be, Will be!

In the sea of people, all
are equal! It really is
simple, life sometimes has dimples!
They don't have to turn into pimples!
What will be, will be!
For us on Planet Earth,
we will all return to dirt!
Ashes to Ashes, Dust to Dust
leaving here we all must!

But, what will be said of us?
When we are gone, will it cause a fuss?
What legacy
will we leave one of thieves?
Will we be lifted in esteem,
or ridiculed, for our very being?
This you or I can't see!
Nevertheless, one thing is clear,
this you need not fear!
What will be, will be!
For, in the sea of people, we are all equal.

Trust and Romance

WE return now to the topic of the predominate romantic, sexual or otherwise, situation on your planet, your home, your Earth. These are the relationships that are between a man and a woman. WE are assured that it will assist you, for this is the reason WE are giving you answers — to assist you. Therefore, whomever you think you should have a romantic relationship with, you can. You will be happy within your relationships, if you venture into them the proper way. WE do not wish to use the word *right* here. For, REMEMBER, there is no right or wrong, there only *is*.

Romantic relationships or any other kind should be based in trust. Is trust given or earned? It is both. You, automatically, give trust. You have no choice. It is there up-front at all times, until one is proven to have taken advantage of your trust, after which time, it must be earned back. First, you must trust yourself and be able to take care of yourself. WE mean for you to love yourself. After this you must be able to love the other or others as yourself. This means to treat them with respect as you should or would yourself, to be able to show concern for their feelings and emotions as you should or would to yourself. This means the ability to give of yourself when sometimes you wish not to. This means to hold your speech, sometimes, when you wish not to.

Contrary to popular belief, this is not disempowering or not taking care of you, as many will tell you. And this is not, not speaking your truth, as many believe. This action is a mere understanding that others have wishes and needs as do you and, sometimes, you can empower them by giving in to your pride and arrogance, thus empowering yourself. This also means that it is acceptable to put your own agenda on the side, if it does not hurt you or others.

Of course, some of you have been taught or learned somewhere that if you do something for another and you don't really wish to, miraculously, WE have observed that some of you feel that this harms you or in some way demolishes your self image. This WE tell you is from the mind of man, IT IS NOT

FROM US. It is impossible to take away from yourself by giving to others, for they are you!

So, WE tell you, if you turn off the TV if asked by your other that the two of you may talk; you will not die. If you say, "That dress looks wonderful on you..." even if you yourself don't care for its design, you will not die, and you are not lying. If you save half of that cookie when you fully understand your other likes the taste of that particular cookie, you will not die, and you are not selling yourself short. If you hold that thought in the midst of anger and rage, you will not bust or explode, and you are not being stepped upon.

Children, please hear US. WE will never tell you anything to hurt you. WE love you; you are US. However, for you to raise your vibrational levels to the point of freedom, misconceptions must be smashed. Most importantly, by acting on what is best for you, you end up doing what is best for others and, most of the time, this will include your beloved, if you have one.

WE know and understand that none of you are incapable, dumb, lazy, or stupid. Many of you just are not remembering who you are. When you remember who you are, you will remember who they are. Then you will come to the full conception of the fact that when you are in any relationship, you are simply doing for someone you love, thus loving your sacred self. If you follow this course, you will be surprised at the return from the universe, US, on this your simple gesture that springs from your love of self.

Therefore, to truly love is to give of your time and energy to your other or others because you wish or desire to.

WE impart to you now that your love should be as so:

Let Your Love Flow

Let your love flow because you wish to empower that one to become his or her highest self. Let your love flow because you wish to cherish them, you wish to uplift them, and you wish to adore them. Let your love flow because you wish and desire to spend time with them, to talk with them, to walk with them. Let your love flow because you desire and wish to laugh with them, to cry with them. Let your love flow because you desire and wish to hold them and to kiss them. Let your love flow so you may enfold them close to your bosom. Let your love flow because you desire and wish for them to fly as eagles towards the heavens and the stars. Let your love flow because you desire and wish for them to be free, thinking for themselves and not robots for anyone or anything, including yourself. Let your love flow because you desire and wish to caress them tenderly when they need your support and backing. Let your love flow because you desire and wish for them to spend silent moments with US alone, apart from you. Let your love flow because you desire and wish to encourage them towards and in their personal and private endeavors as well as the two of yours. Let your love flow because you love them as you love yourself. Let your love flow because you place no unreal expectations on them. Let your love flow because you hold them in the highest esteem and regard. Let your love flow for these reasons and many other reasons. Allow your love to flow because you choose to grow old with them. Let your love be and flow as such.

And as always, send cards and letters. Hug them, believe in them. Encourage them, empower them thus empowering yourself.

However, do not enable them in any attempts by the negative self to stammer or stagger them in reaching the highest vibrational level possible. If you can accomplish these things, you will have a most magnificent romantic relationship or any other kind. You will be honoring yourself. These things you can do, if you but desire and wish to.

Remember, you are the captains of your own ships, which include relationships of all kinds. Most importantly, remember this includes the relationship with yourself, for as you love yourself you draw love nigh to you. This was at one time a secret to many of you on your planet; not any longer. WE have given you this universal truth in plain language for all to understand.

Remember, YOU are creators, YOU are WE, and WE are YOU. YOU are LOVE, YOU are LIGHT and YOU are US.

WE LOVE YOU SO VERY MUCH!"

Matters of the Heart

She came to me trembling,
crying, and sighing.
She swore, "Never Again!
I won't let him in. I do not,
deserve to be treated this way."

This not being the first time
and I suspected not the last.
I listened.
I lay her head upon my lap.
I wiped her tears.
I told her I loved her.
And, as I always do, I informed her,
"Matters of your heart are
up to you!"
Then, just as each and every day,
after the session of her personal
confessions, I sent her on her way,
waiting to open the door another day.

More Than One Romance

Many of you often wonder, can I love more than one person on a romantic level? WE answer this by telling you that you can do whatever you wish, you have free choice. However, can you love each of them as described before? Perhaps this should be the question: And if you answer in the affirmative, can you love yourself while doing so?

WE now have a request of you. Lean towards your mirror and ask yourself:

> Is the behavior I am displaying within this or these romantic relationships allowing me to feel and to know that I AM WONDERFUL and that I AM LOVE?

Will you be able to look in the mirror and say to yourself and US, without a doubt, that you are at your highest vibrational level? If so, continue to do as you do. But, if after a period of time within the life you are living, this current manifestation of yourself, you reach a point where you no longer FEEL good about yourself and of what you are doing, then stop what you are doing and re-adjust.

This may very well be the moment when you are face to face with who and what you really are. For one of the truths you were handed down, one that has not been tampered with too much is from your world's Christian Bible. However, remember that many of your books and reading materials have such truths contained within their pages. The one WE speak to you of now, however, SHOULD HAVE READ AS such:

> "If you speak in the languages of men and of angels, but have not love, you are only a resounding gong or a clanging cymbal. If you have the gift of prophecy and can fathom all mysteries and have all knowledge, and if you have faith that can move mountains, but have not love, you are nothing. If you give all you possess to the poor and surrender your body for others, but

have not love, you are nothing. For, you must come to understand that love is patient and love is kind. Love does not envy or participate in jealousy. Love does not boast; love is not proud. Love is not rude; love is not self-seeking; love is not easily angered and love keeps no record of right or wrong. Love does not delight in harming others but in the truth of the oneness of All. Love always protects, always trusts, always hopes, and always perseveres. Love never fails. Where there is guessing and backbiting it will cease; where there is harsh speech to or of others it will be silenced; where there is misunderstanding there will be understanding."

For WE know and WE tell you all is perfect; therefore, the notion of imperfection will disappear. When you were on a lower vibrational level, you talked as such. You reasoned as such; you acted as such.

But when you obtain a higher vibrational level, you will place those things that serve you no longer behind you. So when you look within the mirror, you will be face to face with God, (US).

Light and Love, WE Are

WE would also bring to your attention that in the philosophy of Ibn Arabi, the ability to see Allah, or (US), in all aspects of the world and life as you know it was fully recognized. Rumi correctly stated, "Love is here like the blood in my veins and skin. He (or US) has annihilated me and filled me only with him/her/(US). His/Her/(US) fire has penetrated all the atoms of my body, of me only my name remains; the rest is Him/Her/(US)." As he died, he summarized his life by pouring out this phrase:

"My religion is to live through Love."

Louise L. Hay, one of OUR daughters once wrote, "I am one with life, and all life loves and supports me. I am deserving. I deserve all good. Not some, not a little bit, but all good." WE implanted this within her mind as WE do with all of you from time to time, words of inspiration and wisdom. WE would add that WE are all of Life, which is Light and Love, and WE do support you and, of course, you do deserve all that is good.

So you must understand and remember that all these words and many more have, of course, come directly to YOU from US. They have come to you through music, poetry, art, literature, dance, and song. They have come to you in philosophy, psychology, and religion. They have come to you with the stars that line the night sky. They come with the rising of the sun each day. They come with the cool evening breeze upon your face.

They come, listen! For all the words that come from US are of love. OUR love for YOU, for OURSELVES. They have come all throughout your human history and will continue to come until all of you return to US.

Remember, your being is not hurt or in pain. You are not designed for hide and seek with self or others on a continued basis. You, certainly, are not designed to cause discomfort to yourself or others. This is the reason why many of your kind don't feel good about themselves. It is implanted in you to be unselfish and when you are selfish or only concerned for yourself and not others, you are in a most unnatural state of being.

YOU are LOVE; YOU are US; WE are LOVE and WE are YOU! Men and women are, by nature and design, pack animals. It is within what you understand to be your DNA to be unselfish. Thus, over time as your scientific community understands, your DNA has been altered. Remember, YOU ARE US; WE ARE YOU and WE ARE ONE.

REMEMBER! REMEMBER!

RE-JOIN US, WE ARE WAITING!"

VI

Spiritual Realms: Angels and Such

The Unseen

Now WE speak to you of what you do not see, but of that which is. WE speak to you of what you think you have seen, or better still, what you really don't see.

Some things you are able to feel, but you cannot see. For instance, an earthquake you may feel; however, you don't see the point of its origin, the epicenter, do you? Unless you were at the epicenter and, if you were there, you most probably would not be reading this. WE ask you what of the wind itself? You may feel it, but you cannot see it. You can only see the effects of it. And yes, there are also of course many things out of your visual field of sight: the person around the corner, the mountain in Europe if you are in Hawaii, and things or locations not in close proximity to you. However, they are there!

So, it is time to explain to you what you have labeled the (spiritual realm) or worlds outside your currently understood plane of existence. There are, of course, other souls and spirits, as you put it "portions of US," the WE that are not in physical form as you understand it. There is a spirit or soul within all matter.

Please hear US. Some are at lower vibrational levels and some are at higher vibrational levels. In plain language, the closer (not in space, in vibration) a soul or spirit is to US, the higher the vibrational level. However, there are items or things you may think are at lower vibrational levels like crystals, which, in fact, are of a higher vibrational level. (With one exception) For now, however, understand that all you survey or oversee in your physical realm — the trees, rocks, all metals, and the paper page or computer screen you are looking at right now — are examples of other forms of visible matter which have a spirit attached to them.

Many are inanimate in appearance and at very low vibrational levels. Nevertheless, they are moving all the time and are conscious beings. With this in mind, be careful of how you treat these conscious beings. All of these may, at one time or another, have been in a physical human manifestation such as yours, or may have been in some other form or another as you call them (lifetime) if they decided to be.

Here it is important to understand WE are speaking of the non-physical as you know it. This includes, but is not limited to, what WE will mention to you within this particular chapter. It would, of course, take up too much space in this book of information to list more than a just a few. What WE do touch upon now is what you are ready to understand and digest.

There will be more information for your remembrance later of course for those who wish to reach higher levels of understanding for the purposes of teaching others. For all that is remembered is to assist you and humankind in remembering who you are. WE are speaking to you at this time to explain the order or breakdown of certain levels of the spiritual realm. WE will speak of those souls or spirits you have named: angels, guardian or otherwise, spirit guides, fairies, elves, Earth elementals, sylphs, undines, gnomes, and, finally, what your kind has termed as "fallen angels" or "demons." WE ask you, at this time, to follow along with US and Remember.

Once again WE tell you that at the start of it all, all were ONE. And still today as you call it, All is ONE. However, ONE is not ONE in totality, which is to say WE are not in OUR compressed form as in the beginning. As it was stated before, when WE decided to split, (the WE included your very spirit or soul), it was the last decision WE made together as one in total completeness. However, your souls and others made and continue to make all sorts of decisions. The only ones WE made since you left are to assist you in returning to the oneness of it ALL. OUR dual purpose is to love you unconditionally in the face of all you may encounter, and to be OURSELVES. It is for US to send out to you at all times light and love. This includes you in your present manifestation and all others you had or may have until the glorious occasion of OUR reunification.

But just as your souls or spirits have taken the physical form to experience life as you know it, WE all still stay together in Light and Love on the limited basis as allowed by the split. As it stands, you create all in your present reality. For example, you created reading these words; WE said "all," for you are created in the image and likeness of WE. WE created and you created your present reality.

(REMEMBER)

Now, other souls or spirits have picked or chosen different realms in which to partake. They have a different calling, a different purpose, and a different reality, and in most cases, a different form other than the one you are experiencing.

REMEMBER, all matter is form, even if you think it is not. WE move ahead for you are ready!

ANGELS

ALL DAY, ALL NIGHT, ANGELS WATCHING OVER ME, MY LORD.

Remember, if you will, the following phrase: "Know not when you entertain Angels." These magnificent words, penned by one of OUR own on Earth, are true. You call that which WE are speaking of now, "Angels." WE call them "a portion of US that are not in physical form" as WE are not.

They choose to assist you in remembering Who and What you are, US. They choose to help you in times you may deem as troublesome. They choose to assist you in times you are in pain and torment. Have you ever thought you were being watched? You are. Have you ever felt you received help from some unseen force? Well you have. Did you really think there was only your earthly human form; that's it, that's all?

There are Angels; WE tell you more angels than you can calculate or guess. There are also too many souls and spirits for you to imagine. These angels are, as you say, supernatural beings. WE will use this term because it is easy for you to understand.

They are not supernatural because they have superpower, for you do too — if you only remember. They are supernatural to you because their powers or gifts are different from yours. They are not in physical form and cannot be, so they, of course, can accomplish tasks other than those you can. They can and have moved items within your physical realm of existence or have caused many of you to lift things or complete tasks that one of you would not normally be able to accomplish during what you term "an emergency situation."

They have no need for food as you understand food to be. You should be able to understand this concept. They have no need for gender, for they do not reproduce. They do not operate as you do, nor do they have a need or desire to.

Be that as it may, they do have a need or desire to help and assist you and this is what they are under contract to do by their freedom of choice. If they are correctly labeled by your religions, they would be labeled as guardians or watchers of women and men. Here your religions, due to the US, have not ventured too far from the truth.

A Vision of Angels

It is important to know, however, that the imaginations of your home, your Earth, are another story. Many accounts of them are incorrect. Understand that you and your kind see what you wish to see, create what you wish to, for you are creators. Therefore, many times what you see is not what is really there. This is the simple and only explanation for the attachment of wings to them, as many of your artists' renditions show angels to have. They or you wish for them to be there. If any of you have the need to feel or imagine that your help comes in some kind of human form with the wings of an eagle, then so be it.

In true reality they come much faster than any bird could or would desire to fly. Please understand also that you too have halos. You call them, "auras." Thus, the halos many of you have given them were a manifestation of the energy field that their being produced.

Further, WE inform you and are telling you that the different personal names and assignments you have given your spiritual helpers are acceptable. It is correct to call them messengers, for they do bring you messages. It is correct to call them attendants, for they do attend to you from time to time, if you so do desire and even, sometimes, when you don't. For, if they desire to give you assistance, so shall it be. It is absolutely correct as you understand correct to be for you to call them guardians for they guard over you and yours with love and affection inconceivable to you at this time.

WE, however, do not send them to guard over each and every individual. They have free choice and watch over whomever they wish and when they wish to. All of you do have many whom attend to you at any given time. Will you recognize them? This may be the proper question. Will you acknowledge their presence or continue to overlook their help as many of you do so often?

If you are on a high vibrational level, you will acknowledge them. If not, you won't. As always, it is up to you. Now, your angel or helper may be called by any of the names you have given them — Michael, Joe, Betty, or Jane; WE do not care. They will help you and so will WE. They are beautiful as you imagine them to be. Keep seeing them as such, if you desire, but know they are just as your mind creates them to be. So WE tell you to also create in your minds that you are wonderful and beautiful, too. Many of you do not do this yet. WE continue to inform you that you are WE. Remember all is beautiful in the known and unknown realms of All there is.

Moreover, they are Holy ones and so are you. But they are not as some of you have called them, "God's helpers;" they are your helpers. WE neither need nor desire any assistance. Since you left the Oneness, you need assistance to recall your proper place with US. With this in mind should you worship Angels? WE say worship what you desire. But would not it be better for you to worship yourselves? For, if you hold yourself in high esteem, are not you holding US and angels as you have called them in high esteem, for you are US?

According to old thought patterns, many of you believe WE spoke to you and humankind directly many moons ago but not now. For some reasons, only known to the ones who thought of it, it was deemed necessary by those thinkers who thought for you, and you allowed such to occur, that angels were needed to speak to you for US. Many of you are, at present, remembering that WE speak directly to each of you all the time. WE speak to you in quiet moments of solitude; WE speak to you in the birth of a child, and WE speak to you in the sound of the rain on your window. WE are always speaking to you as WE are right now within the pages of this book. Yes, there are many times you notice US and far too many times you don't.

So remember, whenever and wherever thoughts of your highest good come to you, it is US. Along with this information comes the fact that the erroneous assignment of your angels speaking for US can be dropped. You no longer need to follow this train of reasoning. Is not this a relief to you? WE speak directly to you and you to US in your prayers. Whenever you call upon US, WE do hear you. Furthermore, WE always answer! However, many times you and many of your kind refuse to listen or accept what WE are telling you.

Finally, when you, as you call it, "die," you do not become an angel. There are enough, a truly uncountable number as you understand numbers to be. You will, however, return in some kind of physical form to complete your contract or to remember more. You will either return to your current plane of existence or come back to whence you came, US, the WE.

WE want you to understand that you may not, necessarily, come back on your planet, your home, your Earth. It could very well be somewhere else. You should also note that the other planets and such in your known solar system are within your current plane of existence. WE wish for you to understand the dimensions of All that which there is. It is simple. Humankind has complicated it. Now, it is time to receive the clear unadulterated truth. Thus, WE continue with more information.

Angels I Cannot See

I know you are there.
I feel your loving stare.
That time I almost died,
I knew you were by my side.
Each night before I go to bed,
I see all you loving angels in my head.
I pray that I remain within your sight,
That you watch over me all night.
That you keep me safe and free!
Doubters say you're only in my head.
But I know, within my heart,
That I and my angels will never, be apart.

Fairies, Elves, Earth Elementals, Sylphs, Undines, and Gnomes

There are, as many of you know, such entities called "elementals" as you have named them, portions or pieces of the All connected primarily to Air, Earth, Fire, and Water. The names you have given these spirits are unimportant. What is important is to understand and realize that they are real as you understand real to be and that what you have tagged as Alchemy is valid. There are, as with angels, spirits that by free choice of their own, during the split WE previously referred to earlier, which decided to become inline, attuned, or to maintain a certain synchronization with the elements of your Earth, other planets, or other planes of existence.

They love the concrete manifestations of your planets as the angels love you, so they have decided to assist the elements in maintaining some semblance of integrity in their relative structures as you understand them.

There are not as many as there are angels. As a consequence of their declining number due to the so-called, "evolution of mankind," they have been overwhelmed on your Earth. WE do not care either way, for you at this time do not care, and as explained before WE are YOU and YOU are US.

It should be noted that WE do, however, have a vested concern for their outcome as should you. What is occurring on your home, your planet, your Earth, the misunderstanding that you must use all resources until there are none left, shall be until you, all or most of you, make a different choice. Possibly you can begin to understand the current condition of your home, your planet, your Earth. Know you this, however, the Earth shall stand forever. The question is, how will it stand? This of course is up to you; you create.

WE do inform you that a physical form is impossible for elementals at this time. But, it was not always the case. Thus, once again, WE remind you that from the mind of man came what humankind thinks or thought they may appear to look like, and that is fine with US. They are your realities, create them as you wish. The mind of man was at one time (immediately after the split) more powerful in and of itself than it is now. (You could move objects with your mind, and complete inter-dimensional travel; these are only a few of the things humankind could do, and will once again do.)

Once upon a time, and this is not a fairy tale, your humankind could see fragments of these beings by mentally forming shapes around their auras. Thus your explanations of their possible physical appearance came to be distorted. You were not seeing the whole image. This is the reason you believed some of them to be small, or imagined them with big heads and pointed ears. Moreover, the aura can not accurately be measured as of yet by mankind; they are, in fact, too large. Your technology has advanced to the point where you may capture a small portion of such with certain luminous lighting and cameras. But, these images are distorted as were the visions viewed by the mentality of man in earlier times.

Now, fairies and such are not restricted to the same laws of gravity as you are. Thus, your perception of their zooming and flying around can be easily explained. They are less massive than you, as you understand mass to be. Therefore, they move faster than you. They move faster than your human eyes can capture their image at this time.

It should be noted that many of your cameras have captured them at certain shutter speeds. They protect the wilds and all within the domain of the animal kingdom, along with all on your Earth not in moveable form as you understand moveable form to be. WE speak here of rocks, trees, soil, and the like.

Overwhelmed

As it stands now, mankind has, as WE informed you, overwhelmed them as you have overwhelmed your Earth. Now, fairies, elves, Earth elementals, sylphs, undines, and gnomes do the best they can with the limited help mankind currently gives them. They are fighting the ways you care for your environment all the litter, dumping of contaminants, cutting down of trees unnecessarily, and raping of fertile lands.

OUR question to you is, "Why don't you help them more?" Many of you are making a beginning. Why don't you? Have more concern for the Earth and what you place within and upon her; have more concern for the water and how you use him. Love the air you breathe as she loves you and continues to give you life. Respect the fire. She is not meant for destruction other than to equalize the forest when it is time to do so naturally. ALL of US will be happy and you will be more in tune with yourselves. The elementals are all around you. Just because you do not see them does not mean they are not there. Know that there are many things you cannot see that are there. You can't see US, nevertheless, WE are most certainly here.

WE reiterate to you that it matters not if you believe these words; they are true. The facts are just as a detective show from your old television days exclaimed, "Just the Facts."

Many of you should remember this.

If you do, help others to remember.

Fallen Angels

This brings US to a touchy subject if, in fact, WE could have a touchy subject. This is the meat of the book. WE have given you the appetizers (where you come from, how sickness has come to be) and the salad (how to improve your relationships along with other important information). WE now give you the main course, for the following is the reason and cause for most of the sad situations as you understand sad situations on your planet to be.

WE are Light and Love — that's it, that's all. Now, just as you chose to be in the physical realm and angels chose to help you or assist you, WE have also explained that elementals chose to be attuned with, what you call, the "elements."

There are other spirits that chose a different course, fallen angels or demons. You have given them many names over the centuries. Most of these names are derived from ancient civilizations and religions (Satan, Beelzebub, Berith, Azi Dahaka, and Abaddon, to name a few). Mankind has given them these supplemental names for the same reasons you have also given the other angels names (you wish to). These names of course do not matter; they are from the mind of man and your choice.

WE wish to point out to you that if you were to correctly tag or label yourselves, WE guess you would or could call yourselves, "fallen pieces" of US. (Pun intended here, Smile!) Fallen angels or demons are very relevant to your present condition and vibrational levels. The present dilemma is how WE can explain this in a way you won't freak out.

Well, first WE will tell you that what WE are about to tell you, you already know. Some of you just choose not to REMEMBER! And, if you do REMEMBER, you try to forget. WE deal in facts, and you have nothing to FEAR — it is, what it is. You have nothing to fear for you are creators and, thus, you can, at any given time, create LOVE, which combats and overcomes all obstacles.

LOVE WILL ALWAYS,

LET US REPEAT, "ALWAYS,"

OVERRIDE FEAR!

Nephilim — A Word You Should Know

Now let US remember there is no devil, never was and never will be, that is except, in the mind of man. And WE already informed you there is no Hell, Purgatory, Death, or Good and Bad. However, writings in the Christian Bible and other historical documentations that refer to a group of beings in the early history of your planet called, "Giants" or "Nephilim" are, unfortunately, NOT A MYTH.

It, therefore, might be a good idea for each of you to grab a copy of the Christian Bible and other non-fiction books that deal with this topic. Many of these tales are not tales at all. You should become acquainted with some of them. All should read the 6th chapter of Genesis in the Bible along with other written descriptions of these ones (giants) handed down through the ages — descriptions such as those found in writings regarding *Jason and the Argonauts*, the *Travels of Odysseus* or *Ulysses* and, *David and Goliath*. They, in a nutshell, briefly informed you of how a large number, as you understand numbers, of what you call angels, changed horses and course in the middle of the stream.

These ones and others of their kind caused much trouble on Earth. It all began when some of the ones who decided not to take physical form, to become angels, to help or assist you in your physical forms, later decided to deviate from their original choice. In the course of their many unseen interactions with humankind, they began to wonder or dwell upon the thoughts of what it would be like to engage in sexual activity with the humanoid form.

Since they are genderless, sexual intercourse with your kind was not a viable option.

But since they, as you, are privileged to have freedom of choice, they changed their minds as many of you do all the time. They decided to cause themselves to materialize into human form. In doing so, they became capable of walking upon your home, your planet, your Earth, for short periods of time and began having sexual relations with human women and men.

You must understand that their physical manifestations could not last at any given time longer than what you understand to equal approximately seventy-two hours. Due to the physical laws of matter, any period longer than what you understand to be seventy-two hours would jeopardize their options and ability to return back to the non-physical realm without totally losing the spiritual freedom that they enjoyed. In laymen's terms, they would die, as you understand death to be, and either return to the oneness of it All or some other manifestation. As explained to you previously, during OUR discussion of death, due to the actions they were engaged in, they most certainly would not at that point in time, as you understand time to be, return to US. To continue, these ones did as they pleased with whomever they pleased while engaging in such sexual activities. As a result of their actions, they were able to father and mother, if you will, offspring or children. It should be noted at this point, that humankind was, at one time, able to de-materialize, time travel, and co-function in two geographic locations at once, prior to having lost certain brain capacities.

Anyway, the children were, because of their unearthly fathers and mothers, born much larger (what you would call giants or in times and language long gone, the Nephilim) than all others on Earth and caused emotional and physical damage to most, if not all, they came in contact with. Once they matured physically, however, they really did not mature mentally as you understand mental maturity to be, for if they had, they of course would not have behaved as they did.

The reasons for their behaviors were due to them being hybrids, or not created or conceived within the constructed order of what are and were natural and normal in your plane of existence. It would be appropriate to say, not within the physical laws set in motion at the beginning of it All. It was a terrible time within your human history. Should you research, you will be able to trace exactly when it did occur. For, there are many records and accounts of the carnages and savagery that transpired during those times. Let us state here that WE understand you don't like to think of this and many of you do not wish to remember. Yet, it did occur, and it is an important part of your remembering process and your Earth's history.

What WE are sharing now with you is the explanation of why WE, the source of All that is, did interfere once with free choice. It was an interference that occurred not within your realm but another. WE will never again do so. WE did it because humankind was, shall WE say, no match for the offspring of these unnatural pairings. WE decided to place a restriction upon those spirits that did participate in the leaving of their chosen realm. They are, forever, banned from taking human form again. Also, WE implanted within the mind of certain of your kind the knowledge and understanding of how to end the reign of the offspring. Thus, they disappeared from the face of your Earth.

Here you must understand, WE are light, WE are love, WE do not judge. However, OUR observation and prognosis of the possible lasting outcome to OUR beloved ones, YOU, set forth our decision and course of action. For, you must fully understand that WE love ALL of YOU, even the ones who caused such a ruckus and disturbance on Planet Earth. Too, understand OUR relationship with you now. Please understand it was not a Judgment; OUR course of action was a needed precaution to preclude anything of this nature from happening again on your planet, your home, your Earth.

Still Interferring — How They Do It

So, as it stands now and forever more in the sands of time, these spirits can not materialize into human form. However, they can interfere and still do. When one of you allows your vibrational level to deteriorate or become lowered, for whatever reason or reasons, these bring to you certain mental thoughts, ideas, and physical actions — thoughts which lead to all sickness, addictions, depression, low self-worth, and esteem, suicidal inclinations, and many more maligned maladies. The above-mentioned are brought about from a vulnerable state of being, opening you up to the influences of these unseen spirits that cannot visit your realm any longer in a physical way, except by way of you. Further, they can be invited into one's being and, of course, many of you do so and suffer the mental and emotional consequences.

Now, how do they do it?

The answer is through thought transference. Thus, they benefit from the carrying out of these thoughts by humans. They are always around you. These spirits attract to those things in each of you that may be negative or not of the highest good for yourself or others. They key into those portions of your psychic being that allow doubt and worry to enter in and, then, find ways to bring about confusion.

They may cause one to worry about money or the finding of love or some external factor that is not really necessary for one's happiness. Some of these unseen spirits are frivolous and will cause little annoyances. When one of you is impatient or dwells upon what you consider to be the imperfections of others, they can and do cause intolerance. This lowers your vibration and brings your personal insecurities and uncertainties up front.

When a negative thought is transferred in your brain by a spontaneous reaction, these spirits wish to cause you to react on the negative thoughts. These negative thoughts are brought to reality when one begins to speak ill of someone. They may start to think of harming themselves or others. Thus, a lowering of vibrational level occurs. Once vibration is lowered, suffering begins. These spirits, thus, become fulfilled. Because of their inability to be physical and to enjoy the fruit of your Earth, they enjoy your not enjoying it. They are jealous, as you understand the word jealous to be, and seek to have any or all of you not happy. They wish or desire for all of you to subject your vibrational level to contagious fear and ignorance brought about by lack of knowledge. Remember this, your higher self knows it.

Let us ask you a series of questions and answer them.

> Have you or anyone you have known consumed alcohol or drugs beyond the human capacity set forth by the laws of physical existence? Why did they not die?

During these times, the spirits that cannot return to your realm supernaturally drain or suck the substances out of humans, thus receiving the effects of what they can no longer experience in the physical realm. On your own time, look into some studies carried out by, what you call, prestigious institutions of higher learning around your globe. Look into scientific studies on the effect of alcohol on the human body. You will run across documented reference materials on various, what mankind has named, "primitive" or "indigenous tribes" who consume alcohol and a substance known as ayahuasca, a hallucinogenic brew made from the bark and stems of the Banisteriopsis vine. These tribes are located in Brazil's Amazon Basin and throughout Africa in Umbanda, Candomble, and other places. The tribes perform ritual dances to the demons. Before they begin, each dancer ingests alcohol and/or the ayahuasca. They chant and dance for a period of time, calling upon the demons. At the conclusion of their ritual, most, if not all, appear to be sober, this is to say no signs or indications of slow reflexes or impaired thinking/actions. Humankind has devised a BAT (Blood Alcohol Test — measures the level of alcohol in the blood or blood alcohol concentration BAC, a level 0.08 — 0.10 or greater is the minimum looked for). Any measurements within these amounts would point towards what you would understand to be "intoxicated." This BAT was administered to the participants before they danced and upon completion. Now, within the physical limitations of your human manifestation, it takes alcohol and the other substances used by the dancers a period of time to be naturally eliminated from the body depending on your weight and other factors.

However, none or "immeasurable" amounts of these substances were found within these individuals. Trust US, WE know all the time frame formulas WE have placed within the mind of man, and the times of these outside quantities of substances leaving the body were not even close.

Can you explain these phenomena logically? Well, WE can and will. The spirits or angels WE are informing you of now drained and did, in fact, thoroughly enjoy the gifts from their dancing benefactors. And they do the same with any of you who may, from time to time, abuse the wonderful gifts your planet, your home, your Earth, has given you for your enjoyment.

A law of the universe and the cosmos is that all things that are to be enjoyed by you should be done in moderation, but each of you already knows and understands this. You may not practice it, but you intuitively know what is permissible for the highest good of your wonderful being. Remember!

WE need to inform you here that the practice of using ayahuasca by any of you who have been told or think you may have some kind of extra special connection to US are misguided. Further, anyone who believes, for one moment, that this substance is somehow designed by US for mankind's use to be nearer to US is mistaken. One of OUR purposes or goals is for you to be in total oneness with US all of the time. Therefore, for clarification, WE are informing you that the use of this substance for a deeper connection with US is nonsense. It should not be done with any regularity or not at all. The choice is yours. This information may upset those of you who have received misinformation. WE, however, tell you the Absolute Truth.

Effects of Lower Vibrations

Additionally, have you ever read in your newspapers, or heard from a friend, or seen on your televisions, someone crazed and confused fighting many of your police persons, ending in a necessity for five or more police to detain such? Have you ever read of or heard of someone who kills himself or others in a most unnatural way, by what you term as "dismemberment" or what you term as a "totally demented form" or fashion? Hear US, they are being influenced to carry out these tasks by spirits not of your realm. It is because they, for whatever reason, came to a low vibrational place within their being and opened themselves up to such invasion. The same holds true for all acts of what you have labeled, "sexual deviate behaviors" or outside of what mankind considers the norm, or anything that has been deemed totally horrible within the mind of man.

These spirits also use other methods to derail one from obtaining higher vibrational levels of consciousness. This can and does occur when one of you, for whatever reason, falls into a low state of consciousness. The low state of consciousness brings about depression, which can bring about compulsive thoughts of low self-worth and esteem. One begins to feel one is a failure, or of no use to anyone, including oneself. This mind set causes confusion in one's thinking. One will become closed-minded towards anything or anyone speaking in regards to hope, love, and the oneness of All. Perceptions become distorted. Anger, along with hostilities towards others, will occur. Thoughts of self-abuse, suicide, and homicide may also occur. The individual will then show signs of hatred and bitterness towards most without any apparent reason. At this point, fear sets in, along with paranoia. Over time, one will become despondent towards society as a whole. The lower vibrational spirits interject rage, panic, and phobias. Guilt and condemnation of self and others ensue.

Behaviors, such as personality changes contrasting from previous normal behaviors, take hold. If you look carefully, you will be able to notice what is known in your terms as a dark countenance falling over the individual: Their eyes will appear dark, black, blank, or maintain a hollow look. They will not be able to look you, or any other fellow human, in the eyes. Further, when one is under the influence of lower spirits, lying, stealing, drug and alcohol abuse may occur. Also, obsession with food, for example, bulimia and anorexia may be manifested. Sexual perversion, irrational crying or laughter may take place at any given time.

When these persons are introduced into any sort of spiritual environment, they will become very uneasy and ready to leave. Language and cutting words normally follow. Abnormal sleepiness and medical problems plague the person — issues such as pain without justifiable reasons, blackouts, seizures, sudden severe headaches, and paralysis. These ones often speak of having knowledge unattainable to others, and they will entice others to join their efforts. Thus, many cults are formed and born of this. Study the histories of cults and see the patterns of those who say they are different or speak of exclusion for them or their followers from society. Be cautious of them.

Those at a lower vibrational level may show the ability to do extraordinary things that do not help to raise the vibrational awareness of others. They may speak of hauntings and of speaking to the dead, which as explained before cannot be achieved within your current realm of existence. This information may also disturb others. WE, of course, do not care! It is their choice and WE speak only the truth.

Concluding this topic WE, All there is, was and ever shall be, tell each of you that WE Love YOU. You are beautiful; you are worthy; you will succeed. None of you are any better or worse than the other, and you are all magnificent. Each of you needs the other; mass global unity is the way. You and all are forgiven because you NEVER HAVE DONE ANYTHING WRONG!

Gifts From Us

At one time you too were capable, and still are, of thought transference (telepathy), so if you really work at it and remember who you really are, you will be able to use this gift from US to help yourself and others. Thought transference was not intended for lower vibrational purposes; therefore, using telekinesis for bending spoon and fork, or levitation to impress others, or for the acquiring of lots of money, is of a lower vibration and it serves no real purpose. If you remember these gifts and do practice them, teach, and help all others to remember and use them also.

Some of you on Planet Earth use the gifts from US only for personal gain and no other reason, or to harm your own kind. When one does, he or she faces the consequences of such actions, for example, poor mental and emotional states of being and what you have termed as "insanity." These actions only cause unnecessary problems. These actions also result in many unnecessary lifetimes on your Earth or somewhere else and prolonged separation from the All. However, it is, of course, your choice.

Here WE will inform you that it is acceptable, or that there is nothing wrong with you or others making a living from your gifts to help others. If, by chance, you earn lots of, what you call, "money," from what you do with your gifts, insure you give much of it away to those in need. Yet, understand that if your gifts harm others or mislead them in any way, it is of a lower vibrational influence and is not in your highest good to continue such. All gifts from US are for the uplifting of your world, your planet, your home, Earth.

Darkness Overcomes Me

Darkness is here inside me.
I see no sun; I hear no birds.
I feel only dread and terror.
Lunacy runs amuck through my
being in a murderous frenzy.
My soul is lost somewhere
in time. Somewhere in days
of youth, I lost my way.
I took this wicked path.
Is it too late to travel
the road of sanity?
To whom can I turn?
Whom can I trust?
Myself? NO!
Committees of devils
dance in my mind nightly.
Fever and suffering overcome
me. I am lost.

Yet, there is good news and cause for celebration. WE have placed within the mind of man/woman an escape or survival plan to get him/her where he/she needs and desires to be, back to US. WE have and will continue to give you ways to repel negative and low vibrational entities and influences. And OUR plan is a most excellent plan and course of action, if WE do say so OURSELVES.

IT IS SIMPLY TO RAISE YOUR OWN VIBRATIONAL LEVEL AND ASSIST OTHERS IN RAISING THEIR VIBRATIONAL LEVELS TO THE HIGHEST DEGREE POSSIBLE TOWARDS AND TO US.

REMEMBER!

Do The Following:

- Acquire and READ mental self-help books.

- Listen to self-help tapes and CDs.

- Learn of and put into practice the healing powers within your body. Begin to understand that you can and do heal yourselves.

- Study and understand the simple way a cut heals. Expand your mind and receive the knowledge that all ailments of human form known to mankind can correct themselves in the same simple manner.

- Learn of your relationships with crystals. They are a form of consciousness; make no mistake about it. They are a part of you.

- Check out acupuncture and see that it can assist your medical professionals in their endeavors to assist you in healing yourselves.

- Study your body's energy centers and the Chakras.

- Investigate the Biofeedback healing device. It has been sent by US for all of you to assist yourselves in healing yourselves and each other.

- Drink plenty of water; it is the Universal Solvent.

- Exercise at home or at the gym; it matters not where you exercise, just that you do.

- You can, additionally, pray as much as you like or not, for WE hear and understand all things said or unsaid. Yes, WE understand all you say and do, even when you don't understand yourself.

- Hug each other as much as you can. Many of you will be surprised at what a simple hug can do. It is powerful!

- Meditate and be in silence with US as much as you can.

- Heal each other as much as you can. Your human touch holds the power of the universe within it. You, each of you, has the power of shall WE say, God, within your grasp. Use it.

- Remember who you are!

In short, Love yourself and all others. It is really why you are, what you call, alive; you are seeking to return to US. When you do these things, when you call upon US, All that there is will come. The Angels will come; WE will come. WE always have and always will.

Most times WE shall come to you in the form of one of your own. WE will implant and send transmissions to their subconscious, information concerning what you are to do. WE will send information on how to raise your vibrational level. WE will help each of you empower yourselves and empower one another. There is never a door closed to you that cannot be opened and all closed doors cause another one to be opened.

REMEMBER THIS; REMEMBER!

WE love YOU. YOU deserve the Best. And YOU shall have it, if you but ask and take the steps necessary to obtain such. WE will help; WE will assist you in obtaining a higher state of being. WE will, thus, help you not allow yourself to be subjected to that which you need not be subjected to. You do not have to be under the control and whelms of the, as many of you call them, "Fallen Angels," or the term WE will use, "your (Fallen Self)."

REMEMBER WE ARE ONE.

WE LOVE YOU!

VII

The Path of Least Resistance

From the time one of you comes into your current plane of existence on your home, your planet, your Earth, erroneous information and misconceptions are introduced into your consciousness. WE wish for all of you to consider a different path, the Path of Least Resistance. This path will raise the level of consciousness on your planet. It will raise the level of vibration. It will bring you closer to each other, thus, bringing you closer to the All, US. This path deals with children and the elderly, for it is written, "when one comes to Earth he or she is helpless and needs others to help them remember who they are. When one is in the twilight he or she is returning to a state of helplessness and requires help to remember they are on their way back to the source of all things." If you do not care properly for these two groups within your society, your society will pass away.

This is the Path of Least Resistance. If you are a man and you have, for whatever reasons, impregnated a woman, and you choose not to marry the mother, support the one who will bear your child. Let her know that she is not alone during the childbirth process. Empower her to understand that even if you and she are not to remain together, you will be there for the child. Make a promise to her, as well as to yourself and to the unborn child. You can do it! You will feel better about yourself, thus, empowering yourself and her.

Once the child is born, be there for them as much as possible under whatever conditions may exist. Continue to interact with the child. Visit the child, spend time with the child, and if you must explain to the child once he or she is old enough for understanding, tell them in a loving manner that you and the mother were not meant to be together, except for the purpose of bringing a wonderful creator into the world.

Never speak ill of the mother. In doing so, you speak ill of yourself and the child. Harsh words of the other were not meant to be, for even if not joined in wedlock, you and the mother will always be one. You or she cannot change the fact that you became one and created one. If you remember to do this, it will cause a lift in the consciousness of the world. Joy and happiness will ensue for all.

If you are the mother, first of all, love yourself. During the pregnancy make the highest choices for yourself and the child within your being. WE do not have to tell you that which is of the highest good, you already understand this. All of you do! But, if you choose to not marry the father for whatever reason, raise the child with love and never speak ill of the father, no matter what. If it be that you must explain to the child once he or she is old enough for understanding the reason you and the father are not together, tell the child in a loving manner that you and the father were not meant to be except for the purpose of bringing a wonderful creator into the world. Harsh words of the other were not meant to be, for even if not joined in wedlock, you and the father will always be one. You or he cannot change the fact that you became one and created one. If you remember to do this, it will cause a lift in the consciousness of the world. This will cause joy and happiness to ensue for all.

If, for any reason, you do not end up or remain with the other due to death, desertion, divorce, or whatever, never speak ill of the other with whom you joined if but only for a moment in time to create a child, even if by rape. For whatever the circumstances may have been, creation took place. Therefore, never speak ill of the other in front of the child. Harsh words of the other were not meant to be, for even if not joined in wedlock, you and the other will always be one.

You or they cannot change the fact that you became one and created one. If you remember to do this, it will cause a lift in the consciousness of the world. Then joy and happiness will ensue for all.

Any of you on your planet, your home, your Earth, whom as an individual or couple (man and woman, man and man, woman and woman, WE do not care), that decides to take one of these little souls as your own through adoption or any other avenue should adhere to the following course. Love and cherish them, protect them from harm, raise them to achieve their highest vibrational level. Teach them not to be a part of any hatred towards others. Never speak ill of the father or mother, no matter what. Harsh words of these others were not meant to be, for even if abandoned by both, they shall always be one with their parents. You cannot change the fact that they became one and created the one now under your care. If you remember to do this, it will cause a lift in the consciousness of the world. This will cause joy and happiness to ensue for all.

Stay Involved during childhood

If, in fact, you and the other are together when the child is born, please do the following, each of you. Embrace the child in the hospital or wherever you may be. Kiss the child, hold the child, and tell the child that you Love him or her. Take the child home and give him/her the best of everything. Give them the best foods, the best clothes, the best toys. Read to them each and every day while they are young. You can do it! Play with them often, encourage them to read and learn, watch movies and TV with them often, walk with them, go on vacations with them once or twice a year. If you have more than one child, choose a night just for that particular child and you. Do this with each one separately, away from the others. Tell them each day that they are special creators and can create a world of love and peace. Teach them how to get along with others socially by your getting along with each of your neighbors. Learn the names of all of the children within a two block radius. You can do it! And if you notice any of these little ones going astray, redirect them in a loving manner. Then, inform their parents of such, thus, empowering them to better oversee their beloved ones.

Upon your children's entering the school system, take an active part. Be involved in what you term the "PTA." You can do it! Visit their schools on a regular basis and learn the curriculum. You can do it! Know all of your children's teachers and friends and the primary personnel at their schools. Go to school board meetings; you are not too busy to do so!

Ensure that your children complete their homework assignments each night before they play or do any other activities. You can do it! Assist them with their homework; it is not too hard for you. All the while, remind your children that they deserve the best that life has to offer.

Talk with your children everyday. Explain to them the facts of life. Teach them to honor their bodies, thus, eradicating those mental states of low vibration which give way to unnecessary human pain and suffering. Let them know that your human form of manifestation is nothing to be ashamed of. Encourage them to exercise and eat properly. Know what music they listen to and know the current singers by name; it is not too much for you.

Most importantly, pray with them, teach them to meditate and meditate with them. Above all, inform them of the love that WE give in the form of freedom of choice. Instill in them a sense of community and respect for Mother Earth. Inform them that prejudices only keep them from higher levels of awareness and consciousness.

THE ELDERLY

Show them by example the importance of caring for the elderly. Teach them that it is written that all those civilizations that did not respect their elders do not exist very long on Planet Earth. The ones you deem as elderly citizens need you. They need your respect first and foremost. They need for it to be remembered that if it were not for them, you would not be! They need for you to remember that they have seen and lived through many times of trial and diverse situations. They need for you to understand that they have forgotten many things that you know not of as of yet. They need for you to care for them; to ensure that they eat properly; do this as if you are caring for a child. They need for you to ensure that they are dressed properly and have security and peace of mind. These ones need not for you to abandon them in aging times. These ones need for you to listen to them, to walk with them, and, yes, to talk with them. They need for you to draw on their past experiences, to ensure that you do not make the same kinds of mistakes. This will ensure that if you make mistakes, they will be new ones. These ones need much more than most of you are currently giving them. They need your time and patience.

There are approximately twenty-two million Americans caring for someone over the age of seventy. You do not need to struggle to help them find the assistance and state of independence they wish and desire. Businesses lose important personnel each year due to employees leaving to care for an elderly loved one. It should and does not have to be this way. You can keep in constant communication with your loved ones even if they do not live with you. Call them and ensure they are out of bed and are taking care of their bathroom activities. Make sure they receive the proper medical assistance necessary to curtail minor health problems before they become serious. This may, also, include the paying for home assistance by a trained professional. You can do it! If you remember to do many of these things, it will cause a lift in the consciousness of the world. Then joy and happiness will ensue for all.

REMEMBER,

REMEMBER WHO AND

WHAT YOU ARE!

VIII

Priorities

The time has come for US to give you introductory information on many subjects. The short concise explanations of the topics, contained within this chapter, are the way these topics stand in relation to the known universe as you currently understand it to be. WE of course have explained to you many times within this text that WE do not dwell within your current plane of existence. Therefore, this information will assist you in having, what you call, a better life within your realm.

Do you desire a better life?

WE desire for you to have one.

If you consider this information, meditate, and think upon it, it will cause a certain Remembrance of whom and what you are, Creators. From this information, WE know that many of you will come to logical conclusions and make your own decision to readjust most, if not all, of the outdated views and beliefs you may have formed. If you follow this course of action, you will most assuredly have a most wonderful life on your home, your planet, your Earth. Further, you will be raising your vibrational level up towards and closer to your higher self. Once this simple information transforms your life, and it will, you will be able to pass it along to others, thus, empowering them to uplift and revolutionize their current conditions and life. They will tell others and as they do so, the consciousness of Planet Earth will rise.

We know you can do it!
Do It, It's Okay.

Hunger

Let US speak to you now of that which you call "hunger." WE ask you in plain language you may understand: Why is this so? WE have ensured there is enough on your planet, your home, your Earth, for all. The eradication of hunger is important and possible. There is no logical reason for this situation on your Earth. Approximately 987 million of your peers are hungry and without proper nourishment. Each year twenty million children will die due to hunger. Hunger alone is a direct effect of a low mass vibrational level on your planet. All of the hungry people on your planet consume less than the minimum calories essential for good health. This situation causes lower mental ability, thus, causing sickness and what you would call unnecessary death. It is your creation, so it is for you to solve.

WE have given you all the tools necessary to fix this matter. Will you? WE will not list the countless ways you as a person and as a society at large can change it. This is a matter for each of you to seek inside self and do something personally about. Of this condition WE will, of course, inform you that there are many things you can do. Therefore, research on your own and do something. You are your brothers' keeper.

Those of you who choose greed and hoarding will, by your own decisions, return to remember once again on your current plane of existence, which of course is not necessary, unless that is what you choose for it to be. Fully understand that there is more than enough vegetation for all to share. There are enough animals for meat and fish and sea dwellers for all to enjoy. There is enough dairy and, surely, enough water. There is enough sun from, what you call, "above," for each and every one of you.

Population

Let us take a look at the land masses on your home, your planet, your Earth. There are seven continents and five oceans spanning over 8,000 miles in diameter. Within the "continents" as you call them, man can and does live any and everywhere he pleases. He lives on islands, mountains, valleys, plains, and peninsulas.

You have been given the two major components needed to sustain life, these two being atmosphere and topsoil, not to mention all the water, trees, and all the other gifts Earth has to offer you. Figure it out for yourselves and make decisions of the highest vibrations.

Land

There is enough land for all. You do not have to be smashed together in ridiculously close proximity, although you are pack animals, which means you thrive on being near others. Still, you have enough room for all to live in a comfortable manner. You may and do have huts, campers, tents, tree houses, boats, townhouses, cabins, single family dwellings, condominiums, apartments, ranches, and many other options. Any type dwelling you desire you may have.

These various abodes point to the fact that you do not have to kill over land. WE have caused it to be that the land belongs to all of you. There is space for all, black and white, Mexican, Italian, Irish, Indian, German, African, Haitians, Canadian, or whatever nationality or ethnic group you may belong to. You can live together in peace and harmony.

All of you know this. But know you this, no one place or spot belongs to any of you, fore mother/father Earth can and will at any given second let you know it is all hers or his. It is important to remember that when man, by chance or by choice, decides to crowd together into one particular place there will be ramifications for doing so in a single location. When any of you jam yourselves together, you begin to deplete the land. Thus, the land will let you know that it is not acceptable that it is being stressed. There will more than often be problems with waste and water management.

Understand that along with overcrowding come traffic jams and other adverse situations. Many of you have experienced these kinds of man-made problems. Therefore, WE inform you that it might be time for the masses or mass consciousness to make different decisions as to where you live and how you treat one another.

WE have also given you the technology to address all these matters or concerns. Remember, WE can't do it for you and WE won't. Therefore, reassess the living conditions and situations in which you may currently find yourself.

Birth Control

WE will now address birth control. All of you already know, because WE have told you, that there is enough land for all, and more. Birth control stems from greed. There are those of you who think there won't be enough for all or that they themselves won't have enough. This mind set has caused you to come up with the idea that the natural reproductive process should be somehow curtailed. So, you came up with a way or ways to alter the natural body functions of male and female. WE wish and desire for you to think long and hard on this question WE are about to ask each of you.

Can there be overpopulation on Earth?

WE will answer this in the next book. WE will answer it, although most of you already know the answer.

Alternative Energy

What do you think?
What do you think?
Yes, you!
I'm talking to you.
What are your thoughts on global warming,
atmospheric and seismographic storming?
What about Sigmund's theories
or your ideas on relativity and
all those new techno possibilities?
Are you a reveler or a simple instigator
without the ability to foresee what might be?
If you joined the human race and ceased
trying to escape.
Escape your duty to we the sea,
the flow of collective consciousness.
What will you do in the midst of the storm,
in early morn,
when the tides turn and the focus is on you,
not the other few?
Tell me what will you do, when the
thinking cap to help our world is placed on you?

Your Earthly Potential

You have the potential to harness and use all the energy needed for millions of years.

Do not be misled; there is enough. There are really countless ways to obtain the fuel you need. Further, there are steps you can take to ensure a cleaner, safer Earth. The Earth, after all, is your home.

The vehicles you drive can be monitored and emissions controlled. You can do it. You can get rid of the gas gulpers; they are outdated. Your automakers are finding this out now. If they do not adjust, they (simply put) will not be around too much longer. People with higher levels of consciousness realize that the days of the SUV are coming to an end. WE of course many times observe with wonder those ones among you who live in cities and drive off-the-road, four-wheel-drive cars and trucks that never go off the road.

The good news, however, is that many of your auto companies are beginning to produce more cost-effective environmentally friendly vehicles. Hydrogen-fueled and Natural Gas-fueled vehicles can be used. Hybrid Internal Combustion Engines and other clean burning alternative fuels are and will be made more available to you. (There are vehicles that run on air, yes air. Find out about them, refine them, and use them). WE are telling you of these advances. Read up on them. Talking to each other will bring about motivation to make vehicles more cost efficient. The time is coming; WE have made it so; the future is here.

WE have placed within the mind of man all that is necessary. If you listen to your inner genius and adjust, carbon dioxide, carbon monoxide, and nitrogen dioxides will be reduced, thus curtailing smog. Exhaust emissions will be lowered.

WE have implanted these ideas in your minds, so use them for the betterment of your home, Planet Earth. You live in your plane of existence, WE don't, but WE love you and will always give you a way out. And, of course, it is your choice, and, as always, WE are watching.

Global Warming

Tropical Lesson

The frogs and mosquitoes, leaves
greener than green, waters trickling
down the falls.
Monkeys swinging on ancient vines,
mud stacked by tropical rainfall.
Everything, the anatomy of the jungle,
Even the souls of the Ancestors knew.
But not us!
The fruit flies, the ants tunneling downward,
they all Knew!
We on the other hand, we had no conception.
We failed to see,
the tribulation that Mother Earth
was on alert!
Unbeknownst, We came, to uproot, disturb,
    the equilibrium.
As we always do!
We were destroying our protection without
any reflection,
or discernment.
A lesson we missed.
The Hazards of Man!

Earth Crying, Dying!

It is the rain falling, calling.
Calling to the universe begging, pleading Help!
I am dying. I am crying.
I am sending forth my tears into the wind.
My children do not see what they do to me.
Are they unconscious of the confusion,
the disillusion of oil spills on me?
Can't they see?
It was not meant for me to house, within my bosom,
bombs things of destruction.
Am I falling from grace?
Do not they understand the demand
they place on me, if simple rainforests cease to be?
What of the tree? What of the grass each time
the guns flash?
What of the misuse of my land,
the building of cities on quick sand?
Tears flow from me.
Children of the Earth,
wake up to see, what you do to Me.

WE would like to address what you have named, "Global Warming." WE did, in fact, inform you earlier in this communication that the Earth as you know it will stand forever. Your home, your planet, your Earth, however, goes through cycles. As your Earth goes through its changes, there are many steps you can take to make things easier.

Make changes in your homes. Buy energy-efficient appliances. Turn down water heater temperatures. Use compact fluorescent light bulbs. Install double-paned windows and search to find out more steps you can take. These things will help. Remember, it is all up to you.

The changes WE speak of have happened since the Earth's creation. What WE are relating to you now is no doomsday scenario. Rather, it is your day/future scenario. Yes, the thickness of the ice in Greenland, and what you call, the "polar caps," is depleting. It always does over time, every 11,500 years or so. The rotation of your planet in the solar system, as you understand it, brings about a certain relative position which places it in perfect alignment with all others, as you know them, heavenly bodies. When this anomaly or what you may consider irregularity occurs, your home, your planet, your Earth, warms up. Temperatures in your atmosphere rise and carbon dioxide levels change. Mind you, this will go on for many decades.

There are a few who follow your climate changes; seek out their counsel. There is, also, much information that will be able to inform you of your planet's past. Do research! During the times in the past history of your planet that WE are referring to, those animals or species that were unable to adjust simply disappeared. Animals, such as, some species of rhinos, some distant relatives to the elephant, apes, pigs, and rodents became unable to adjust to the rising temperatures and became extinct during Earth's warming. During the time of global freezing, Bison, Wooly Mammoths, Cave Bears, Cave Lions, and many Spotted Hyenas either disappeared totally or disappeared from certain ecosystems. It is what it is.

The process WE are referring to that is underway now, "warming leading to freezing," is at its beginning stages. It is important for you to understand that man has nothing to fear. Adjust and keep on keeping on. Man can and will adjust. Use your thinking caps. WE like that previous phrase. It is, of course, from US.

Do what you need to do. WE have implanted within the mind of man the ideas and concepts that will get man through this time of re-adjustment. Some of your occupied land masses, habitations or settlements in coastal areas will become covered in water in the places you call Europe and North America. Just move on inland and all will be well, if you take OUR suggestions. If not, many lives will be lost. After the melting down, so to speak, comes the freeze. Yes, another mini-ice age. However, once again WE have implanted within the mind of man the ideas and concepts that will get him through this time of re-adjustment.

THIS WILL NOT OCCUR IN WHAT YOU TERM OR CALL THE, "NEAR FUTURE." WE FULLY UNDERSTAND THAT THERE ARE THOSE OF YOU WHO WILL TRY TO MANIPULATE THE PREVIOUS STATEMENTS TO CAUSE UNNECESSARY FEAR. HOWEVER, WE WILL MAKE IT CLEAR THAT NONE OF YOU WHO ARE ALIVE NOW IN CURRENT HUMAN FORM WILL WITNESS THIS, NOR YOUR CHILDREN AND, POSSIBLY, NOT YOUR CHILDREN'S CHILDREN.

Please do not allow fear to cause inactivity on your part. Many frightening views have been put out to spread fear among you. Some of them may happen. Whatever does happen, your kind will survive. Yes, the Australian continent is becoming dangerously dry and snow caps are melting on many mountain peaks. Some say that glaciers will disappear. Know there will be new ones. They point out that many sea dwellers will be no more — this always happens and will continue to. However, there are more sea dwellers than you know; you will always have fish in your seas. And by the way, man cannot over fish.

It is also a fact that man does destroy far too many trees which affect the rainforest, thus causing a threat to many people on Earth. WE tell you, you can make a higher vibrational decision to stop cutting down so many of your friends, for they are your friends. Trees keep your air safe for you to intake. And of course all of you can stop the mass pollution that clutters your waterways.

> Note: The above section, printed bold was added, for the one who is writing this material for US, for YOU, for WE, began to allow his imagination to take him into fear; some unreal scenarios of doom and gloom. This caused an unnecessary pause in what you are reading now. WE had to calm his spirit before he was able to continue. This took two of, what you call, "weeks." It was, of course, his choice. Everything WE have just related to you can and will be overcome by man. WE are confident in man's abilities to adjust and sustain mankind. And of course WE are waiting. WE are watching. WE are cheering you on and so are the angels that come to each and every one of you all the time to assist you.

Glacier

From the cruise ship I saw you.
Your mass, your form, extending
from high then descending below, captured me.
You were ever moving, yet still.
Your colors were a mix of octamerous lights.
Awe and wonder overtook my being.
I watched.
Your fog-covered top gave you the
appearance of an icy god.
The accumulation of ice,
of cold,
sent chills through my mortal soul.
With you I felt joined as one.
Your inner mysteries were a shocker to me.
What lay within?
As shive and splinters of your bounty floated past,
a question came to me.
What would a highball taste like, surrounding
a piece of you?
As ship drifted away I stared. As steam rose I wept.
I would miss you, my friend. Under current
conditions, you will be gone in ten years.

Money

WE shall now speak with you of that which you call, "money." What a wonderful basic concept and it should be; it came from US. Well, the idea of it anyway. Money is some unit used or accepted as payment for goods and or services. You also use it to pay off debts. None of you really owns anything. Therefore, to charge another for something is from the mind of man. Well that's another book, another time. You have constructed it to be used as a unit of exchange. As you know, it is only paper, ink, or some metals you have chosen to use. The first remembered mints were in Rome, although there were others. WE also give you a history lesson while sharing this information with you. The civilization that studies past times and learns from them will survive. (Hint)

Money was created to be used, so use it. Go ahead and spend it. Make as much of it as you can, buy with it, roll in it, play with it. But let it not consume your being! Know and understand it is only a means to an end, that's all. The more of it you get, the more you should give away. It will come back to you, for it loves you just as you love it. You are, after all, its creator.

You can have as much of it as you like. Why not? As one of your sayings goes, "You can't take it with you," and, rest assured, WE don't need or want it, nor do the angels or your brothers and sisters on other planets in other realms. They have their own forms of, what you call, "currency." Some of theirs looks better than yours. (Smile, don't be so serious!) WE have explained to you before that you may have as you desire. Just call it into being, make it so. All of you can do it! And, this is not a secret. If you desire it you can obtain it.

The question is, "Do you desire it? Do you really desire it?" Many of you say you desire it, but do nothing to receive it. Yet, if you really want some money, lots of money, take and carry out the steps and actions necessary to get it and keep it. There are many on your planet, your home, your Earth, that will, in fact, help you get it. You have all seen those fabulous infomercials on how to obtain or make money, try some of the suggestions; you may well be surprised and you might even make some money. Most of the people who make the infomercials don't want any of your money, other than what you may pay for the information.

They do, however, want their own. They understand there is enough money for all. Seek these ones out; they are all around you. They write books about how to obtain money. They give seminars on ways to gather it. You can, too, if you want to. And WE will assist you; WE always assist you, if you but ask. Then listen for an answer. WE will even give you a heads up. It is not a good idea, as you understand ideas to be, to ask others for monies that you do not really need to sustain yourself. Therefore, take only a minimal amount for your services.

Do the following:

1. Exclaim out loud to US, the universe, yourself, how much money you want.

2. Visually view money as often as you like.

3. Make a plan to obtain it, a plan which harms no others or yourself.

4. Do what is necessary to obtain it. Some work will be necessary, however you decide to do it, but do it.

5. When you get it spend it. Buy whatever you desire while remembering you must, however, continue the above four steps on a consistent basis and save to ensure you can continue to carry out your plan.

6. From your surplus or excess, give a lot of it away. It will come back to you accompanied by more.

WE shall, at this point, share with you that the above are laws of the universe not written with pen and paper. These laws are written in the sun and moon and the very air you breathe. They are written in your heart and in your mind. If you follow them, any material objects desired shall be yours, if you truly desire it to be. However, if you neglect any of the above, you may not get what you desire. Instead, you will receive that which you put out to receive. And, of course, if you are operating from your higher self, all will be well. WE desire all to be well, don't You?

Remember, WE Love You!

More

I want more, more money,
more excitement, more women.
I want more, more work, more pay,
more play. More sun, more fun.
I want more, more laughter, more
cars, more shoes, more pants,
more jackets and more furs.
I want more diamonds and pearls.
I want more, more music, more
trains and planes.
I want more,
more joy and peace.
I want more to eat and more to drink.
I want more, more sleep.
More pie, ice cream and cake.
I want more, more moon, more stars.
Give me more, more to explore and enjoy.
Give me more toys,
more vacations, more satisfaction.
More sex, more love.
Give Me,
More, More, that's what I'm looking for!

Politics

Manifesto of Youth

The young man said,

> "I will heal the sick, feed the poor.
> I will give of myself to my brothers.
> I will be a transmitter of hope and joy.
> I will comfort the elderly.
> I will protect all creatures on God's green Earth."

However he was young,
he couldn't understand,
to accomplish such things, you must be one hell of a man!
You have to practice every day,
to stay that way.
Therefore, time elapsed and his simple Manifesto simply Collapsed.

WE shall speak with you of Politics and conditions of Governments. Although WE do not live within your current realm of existence, WE do have a vested interest: you.

Since the beginning of what you now know as documented history, His-story, Her-story if you would like, WE don't care, someone or a group of some ones had to take the lead. This is the way it is, "it is what it is," and WE like this saying of yours. This was placed within your sub-conscious being by US, by You. It was placed there for survival of the species. Even at that time some of you had inklings of remembrance. You, intuitively, understood that there must be order and reason. The universe is order and reason. WE are order and reason and so are You. Man is, as you have discovered, a pack animal. Try as you will, try as many of you might, when you are alone for long periods of time, insanity comes; it always does. You were not meant to be alone. Let US move on here.

Someone had to say in whatever languages you used then, "Let us stick together lest we are taken by the elements alone. Let us huddle together and draw from each others' strengths." Now, this one or ones were your early leaders or at that time, crude governments. As long as they acted and behaved in a manner that took into consideration their higher selves and the higher selves of others, all was well. However, the minute, the second they began to think of only their own selves and personal gains, and that possibly they should have more than others without giving others the opportunity to have the same as they, allowing ego, distinguishing themselves from others on a level other than a mere different physical manifestation or thinking they may be better or superior to others, problems began. Remember, All are Love, All are the same, and All are US.

Therefore, WE impart this to you now, for now is what counts. Titles such as, "President" and "King" or "Queen" are, of course, up to you. If one of you endeavors to be a leader, it matters not what political party, as you have named them, you are associated with.

Lead with Power as follows:

First, understand True POWER. As you say on your Earth, "people are drawn to power," but you must remember: Power is not a birthright, a reward of military actions or political victories. Power is spiritual and, if misused, will turn on you. Power is the result of having a positive influence on others. Real power results from having the strength to overcome lower vibrational influences on all actions that may affect yourself and others.

WE tell you, those of you who seek power, that love family, and remember that making efforts to ensure good health for all is the path to obtaining that power. WE tell you what "Real Power" is. It gives positive positioning to all, positioning that allows all citizens to grow and achieve higher vibrations.

This power is not ambition; this power enables others and yourself to obtain excellence. This power promotes growth for all. This power entails communication and observing the needs of others. This power causes no others to feel helpless or alienated. This real power allows the person in power the ability to be talked to and reasoned with at all times. This power has a level of integrity that serves as a model to others.

Self-knowledge is power — the knowing and understanding that you are a creator and that all others are also. Real power has no struggle. Therefore, if you seek political power and leadership on your home, your planet, your Earth, treat your entire scope of constituents as you wish to be treated. Be fair to all whom have, by vote, which is free will, placed themselves under your authority and rule. Ensure that those who look to you for guidance have the same chances and choices as do you. Ensure that all may prosper, that all are equal. If you accomplish this, it will return to you and you will be loved and admired for understanding that all of you are the same. Each of you whom aspire to be a leader is capable of this.

Those of you that may live in a country where your leaders are not working as described above should Replace them. You can do it and you and all concerned will be better off. There is really not much for US to say in regards to this matter. You already know these things. Remember them and all will be well. Further, Remember: Simplicity is the Key to all in your known and unknown universes and that although all may appear to be complex, all is really simple.

Any politicians at local or international government levels who do not meet and maintain these simple prerequisites should be removed. If they appear and are, in fact, in distress over your decision to oust them, tell them to speak with US in prayer, and in moments of solitude reflect on their past actions. After a period of time, they will understand, for they will be speaking to their inner selves. Make no mistake about it, inner self knows what is appropriate to do at all times.

Know that Conditions, some of which were mentioned before, such as famine, war and peace, global warming, issues of personal freedoms, and violence are, in fact, easy to solve. WE will never interfere in these matters, they are yours. Once again, WE reiterate to you that the issue you have named, "Abortion," is totally up to each of you and the fetus on an individual basis as are all decisions you may make. No-one in all the known and unknown galaxies has been given the authority to tell you what to do with your own bodies and no one can judge you. Remember this, however, deal with all situations that may cross your path at the highest vibrational level possible.

At this place within the information that WE are presenting to you, WE wish to speak or touch upon the following question:

Is one nation protected by God over others?

The answer is "no." All nations man has formed and the entire Earth is protected by All that there is, was, and ever shall be. However, know this, any nation or its peoples that do not seek the highest good for all, which is within the constraints of universal laws, and do not, to the best of its ability, protect and care for others as they would themselves, all of its citizens, will not stand for too long. You will see to this, not US. And of course WE would have it no other way, WE do not Judge.

In reference to mankind's past history and dealings in matters of war and peace, to say the least, your record on your planet, your home, your Earth, has been poor. Understand that WE mean, "poor," in regards to the way recent governments, which are a collection of individuals, have dealt with situations such as those involving Hitler, Hiroshima, Nagasaki, Vietnam, Belfast, and, most recently, anything to do with Africa, Iraq, Iran, Palestine, and Korea. Now the question is, "Will the mass population of your planet, your home, and your Earth react with higher vibrational behavior in, what you call, "the future?" Will the mass consciousness rise to the occasion, and void the decisions of a few self-seekers who call themselves leaders?

YOU CAN! WILL YOU?

RELIGIONS

WE shall speak with you of Religion. Possibly, this subject should be read by those of you whom are of the Christian, Buddhist, Islamic, or any other faith. It is important for all of you to understand that these wonderful Religions in their basic fundamental, primary beliefs are correct. There is only one God. WE are a conglomeration of All there is, moreover, not singular. However, the inherent idea of religions, that getting to know and understand US, All that there is, was, and ever shall be, is acceptable. There is nothing wrong, as you say, with wanting to get to your roots and to understand on a deep level the meaning of, what you call, "life." WE know this is good, as you understand the word good to be.

This is, therefore, the main reason WE are transmitting this information to you. WE wish and desire for you to know US better, as well as learn more about yourselves at the same time. WE implanted, within your sub-conscious mind, the thirst and need to understand what you do not know. WE wish and desire for you to understand what your life is as WE understand it. WE wish and desire for you to Remember.

All throughout time, what you do not understand, you have made up. However, when what you make up is harmful to self and others and misinformation comes into play, WE have a problem, All of US. Unfortunately, WE have had a problem for some time now, actually for many centuries. Many of you have based many of your concepts about who and what WE and you are in Fear and this will no longer do.

Many Religions help and have helped millions change their lives and come to a higher vibrational level. They have assisted many in beginning the remembrance process. This is good, once again as you define the word "good." Many Religions have caused and helped to cause many to change and to become better humans, become more aware of who and what they are. If, however, the main goal of a Religion does not include all without restriction, they are not representing US. If their particular concepts and practices do not include equality of all members, or if those beliefs are not fully of Light and Love, it causes many to fall by the wayside, and, of course, this is not from US, All there is, was, and ever shall be.

You now have and, for some time, have had many constructed or painted versions of US within your reality that are tainted and really unbelievable portraits of US. Many of these ideas fully misrepresent who and what WE are as well as who and what you are. Many Religions and denominations have chosen to exclude others and place unnecessary restrictions on freedom of choice, and this will not do.

WE spoke with you, previously, of the variety of names you like to call US, and of course, all are fine just as long as you call and communicate with what is essentially your inner/outer self. Precociously and precariously, many of you have turned us into some kind of monster; an insecure, manic, narrow-minded, narcissistic entity. This is what you have made US out to be, much to OUR chagrin.

Therefore, WE put forth a series of questions and answers to each of you. WE wish and desire for you to ponder long and hard on what WE are presenting to you now. WE, further, ask that you discuss these with your friends and all you know or may come into contact with on your home, your planet, your Earth. These questions and answers may help you to remember some important missing pieces. These questions may help you understand more clearly that WE are not a vengeful, killing judge of those who go astray. WE do not have an appetite for you to blindly serve US.

WE do cause miracles. However, most of the time, the miracles come through one of you, sometimes through many of you, as evident in the recent elections in what you understand to be "America." It was a miracle performed by the mass consciousness of that country. This consciousness is a sign of the raising of vibrations on your planet, your home, your Earth. This wondrous consciousness from US, allowed the inner being of many to overcome fear and poisonous prejudices. It, allowed the masses to place collective hatred aside. The universe sang in jubilation. WE sang, for it was the highest vibration of US at work. Lower portions of US did not influence the majority. WE always sing when man and womankind act in their highest good. You must further understand that WE are not bias culturally or nationally. WE are available to all people of all cultures. WE are not limited unless limited by you.

WE did not become flesh only once. WE are all of you; you are OUR flesh. The image of US changes with each generation and WE do not care. The Bible and the Quran are two of the millions of books WE use to touch you with the written word. WE touch you with architecture, music, art, drama, and things that go beyond reason as you understand reason to be. WE live in Mosques and Churches, huts, and caves. WE are creation, wisdom, scripture, philosophers, and values. WE are in the natural world and the not so natural. WE are survival and hope. WE speak through your bodies and your intellect. WE are everywhere, yet, nowhere, yet, now here. WE are found through-in and throughout. WE are the natural order of things seen and unseen. WE are the aboriginal death and life. WE are not sacrifice, unless the sacrifice is for you and all connected to you to obtain the best. WE are your memory, but we dissipate as smoke. WE are associated with the moon and the stars. WE are related to all things, yet unrelated at the same time. WE are increasingly human, not heavenly. For, what is heaven, except where your heart and soul dwells.

All of these words WE impress upon you for you to think and remember. It is easy to have access to US. In fact, it is impossible for you not to have access to US. Don't you see; don't you feel OUR words to you? WE do not remain in dead bodies. WE are of the living, the walking, and the talking. WE are intoxicating to be with, are WE not? Think of the times when you are alone, looking at the sky, smelling the grass, or playing in the snow. It is US. WE are the powerful producers of your dreams, through you and your actions.

WE do not enter into you when you accept US, as you have been told. WE are always inside of you. WE are not a deity, except in your mind. WE are pure energy enhanced through meditation, prayer, hard work, and love. WE do not need a worshipper. WE need a lover of self and others. WE need someone who is like you, full of worry one moment and laughing the next. WE are coming to you in this manner and at this time to assure you that many of the constructed thoughts of US are not US.

WE are simple. Yet, WE are complicated. It is from and within your mind and imagination that WE have a need for your concocted elaborate, and long, drawn-out ceremonies and services to be pleased. All the images and metaphors used by you and your religions make US happy. But, WE are telling you, "WE need them not."

Religions have set up and carried out many actions, supposedly in OUR name. These actions were perpetrated by past and present religious fractions that have hurt so many of you. The shame is, all of it was due to fallacies and a quest for power by a few. These few brought up a notion that some of you have a clearer pathway to the oneness of it all and that they should be the only ones listened to and that you should also give them your hard-earned monies. WE tell you, however; that just the words, "Hi, I know you are there," turns US on more than a thousand voices singing praise. For, OUR joy comes from you singing to and for one another. Did you know that a simple smile causes 57,000 lower vibrational fractions of US to flee you? Well, now you do!

WE have gone on long enough. WE get carried away speaking about OUR love affair with each of you. Please, now take a look at the questions WE place in front of you. They, of course, come from US and from YOU!

Why would WE require you to worship US in adoration?

Adore yourselves and all others.

Why would you need to build entire institutions around learning what WE say?

For what WE say and have said, WE say it to each of you, each and every day, wherever you may be.

Why would WE test you, or cause you to be tempted by something opposite of US?

Your life is not a test. It is your life, the full experience of whom and what you have made yourself to be with the help of many others.

Why do you need holy water?

All water is holy as are all things on your Earth, including each one of you.

Why must you bow down to US?

Bow down to no one. What are you bowing for? WE wish and desire for you to stand-up. It is in your highest good to stand-up for self and all others. Each of you should, however, look all of your kind in the eyes. Face to face and, see self. Therefore, stand erect in front of US and all others. Speak your truth to all in a gentle, yet firm, manner.

What is a holy man or woman?

All are holy.

Why would WE sanction any war?

WE do not sanction war or killing; you do. Don't place it on US, except for the fact that we are connected by time and space. However, once again, WE do not live in your known world. WE have not war or killing. Further, no war can be holy, save the fact all is holy, yet not sanctioned by US, only observed. If one of you makes a choice to kill yourself and others in what you have named a "suicide bombing," Hear US Now, for WE are what you deem as Allah or God; WE tell you, you will not be blessed or given some special place in, what you call, "Heaven." You will suffer another human manifestation on your Earth or some other realm for making a decision that was not in your highest good or the highest good of others. Why would any of you think this would be acceptable? WE are not mocking you. You are mocking US.

Know this: Whoever may have, for whatever reason or reasons, passed the information on to you that it would be in any way a high choice to do the above mentioned was, and still is, unless they have recanted such, under the influence of lower vibrational pieces of the universe. Please remember Who and What each of you are, Light and Love, US.

Why would WE send plagues upon what is essentially OURSELVES?

Things happen for you have created and caused most situations on your home, your planet, your Earth. You have caused such through carelessness, neglect, and other forms of not being in touch with your higher selves. Can't put it on US.

Why would WE hide the truth from any of you?

Ridiculous, WE won't even address this further. You think about it, talk to each other, and remember who you are.

Why would WE create a Hell?

Once again, that is Ridiculous. WE would not.

Why would WE turn people into pillars of salt?

If WE could "laugh," as you have named it, WE would. This is a funny one.

Why can only a chosen few serve US?

Well, none of you have to serve US; WE don't need anything as you understand it. Serve yourselves. So, all may serve US, if you wish. What would you give US?

WHAT IS SIN?

Something made up in the mind of man.

WHAT IS RIGHT AND WRONG AND WHO DECIDES?

No such things, only concepts. Why don't you guys and gals talk about this one without killing each other? (Smile)

WHY WOULD THERE BE ONLY ONE CHOSEN PEOPLE?

HA, HA.

WHY WOULD WE CAUSE A FLOOD TO CLEAN UP THE EARTH?

What? However, to give you another example of how one of the books given to man and womankind was twisted, WE set forth this. There was a man named Noah. He did build an extremely large ship for surviving a regional flood that occurred in his day and time. He was given information from guardian angels on how to survive. Yet, the flood was not global; he misinterpreted it to be global. The fact is, it was global to him.

Remember, your kind believed for many years that the world was flat. Moreover, the flood was not to clean up sinning humans. WE have already addressed how the giants or Nephilim of old were eradicated. Yes, many of them did "die" as you call it during the flood. Furthermore, many others survived who were not known to the man Noah.

WHY DOES ANYONE HAVE TO SAY, "HAIL, MARY" THREE TIMES, OR AT ALL?

If you wish to find true love, say "new kisses" thirty-seven times and call US in the morning. HA, HA.

WHY WOULD WE WISH FOR YOU TO DENY YOURSELVES OF LIFE'S PLEASURES?

Would not abusing them be enough?

WHY WOULD WE CREATE A PLACE CALLED HEAVEN?

This is also from the mind of mankind.

Why would the streets of this Heaven be gold?

Why not silver?

Why would WE be jealous of anything or anyone, including the other God names you have constructed in your minds?

If you really think about it, they are all US anyway.

These are just a few of the questions WE would like for you to think of. WE, of course, could lay out more just as silly as these. What WE are relating to you is this: Have your places of worship, but let no man or woman tell each other what one of you must think or how one of you must act to please US. WE are always pleased.

Allow others to examine the books and doctrines you call "scriptures" for themselves, and any other reading materials they wish to, without disapprovals or reprisals. Teach each other that all of you have and will make some decisions that are not in the highest good of yourselves and others, and that a new day gives rise to corrective actions. WE, therefore, approve of all of your religions for WE approve you.

Are WE to ask you not to think? Then why would you have such a magnificent brain? WE can't be displeased. WE are Love and Light, pure and simple. If you must have chapels and such, let them all be for the teaching of love and light. Allow all to enter and leave as they like. Make no requirements for membership other than desiring to be in communion and friendship with you. If one of you misses some or all of, what you call, services/meetings, or makes a mistake, or some mistakes, don't ban or excommunicate the person. WHY? Are not you in the business of healing and mending broken souls? With some of your so-called religions, WE can't tell by the actions of the members that they belong to the religion. WE are not judging them or the religions, WE are making an observation.

In other words,

If you preach love,

Practice it.

Did not WE place within the mind of one of you to write something like (forgive seventy times seventy)? One should forgive anything and everything, for none are to judge. What is judging? Within the walls of your religious establishments explain that each and every one of you is US. There is no other truth. You don't need one person to bless you. Rather, bless each other and yourselves by your words and actions, carried out to the highest vibrational level possible at all times. No one person or place can contain what WE are. However, everything contains what WE are.

Remember!

Here for you now are what you should name, call, or deem:

The Absolute Truths With One Repetition

WE are All there Is, Was, and Ever shall be.

WE love you, you are Us and WE are you.

Freedom of choice is the greatest gift there is.

WE never interfere with freedom of choice.

WE speak Absolute Truth.

WE do not control.

WE do not punish.

WE do not correct.

WE give loving truth and guidance.

Freedom of choice is the greatest gift there is.

WE will always inform you of what is in your highest good, either by placing it within your subconscious mind or causing someone to tell you.

Our dear beloved ones, these are the Absolute Truths of your reality, anything else is not. You may believe them or not; you have freedom of choice. However, know this, whatever you do, think, or say, these are the Absolute Truths with one repetition; you cannot change this fact.

Spiritual

All throughout, what you call, "time," some have understood and remembered that all is spirit. Many of you are now remembering such. You are spirit; WE are spirit. You are a spiritual being in a physical state of being. What is spirit? First, let's examine what the mind of man has come up with. Within one of your humankind dictionaries, it is written that spirit is: Breath, a life-giving force, and that it is mysterious or of an unknown nature. The same dictionary relates that spiritual is: anything relating to, consisting of, or affecting the spirit or sacred matters, and that it is of ecclesiastical rather than lay or temporal.

Some of this description is correct. Spirit is breath and life-giving. But WE tell you it is not mysterious or of an unknown nature. Simply put, Spirit is you, all of you, the walking and talking. All of you are Spirit, US. WE have, of course, observed many of you throwing the words "spirit" or "spiritual" around. Throughout history this has caused great confusion and misunderstanding.

Many of you, incorrectly, believe that spirit or spiritual deals only with the divine or what you consider US to be. Now the intellectuals among you say that the spirit is restricted to or exclusive to the outer realm or non-physical forms. Some believe that the soul of a man or woman is separate from one another. WE tell you that they are one; there is no separation. All is unity and all is together, which means all is spirit and all is spiritual in nature.

There is a spirit in every task that each of you undertakes everyday. There is a spirit in cooking, cleaning, or swinging a hammer. For, remember, all is connected and not apart. This means that there is a consciousness or spirit that flows in and around all. Thus, when WE speak of mass consciousness, WE are speaking about a majority of you on your home, your planet, your Earth.

All throughout this book, WE have shared the fact that all is together, therefore, the theme remains the same. You may not wish to admit it, but even the most prejudice amongst you knows within the inner being that his or her thoughts of superiority are misguided. They won't tell you, but the spirit that WE are talking about now intuitively understands this universal truth.

Some religions have taken it so far as to tell you that one person showed a personification of pure spirit. WE tell you all of you do. There is nothing mysterious about you or US. You are light and love, breath, life-giving, and sustaining, transfixed into a body, a human manifestation. Spirit cannot be seen or touched as you understand seeing and touching to be. However, spirit is felt and known or understood to exist or to be. You can, of course, not see the breath unless certain conditions exist; you know what they are. Further, all is known to you. Only recalling or remembering is needed.

Now, you have been taught or told and have chosen to buy into the idea that some things are more sacred than others. Most of this misguidance comes from your early churches and religions; the idea that lay persons, who for reasons only known to the folks who made it up, lack extensive knowledge or understanding of spiritual matters. This idea was constructed by money-hungry power seekers who desired to keep the masses in darkness and disease. It should be noted by most of you that they succeeded for many centuries until many began to remember the truth of it all.

But, how can you become more spiritual? Be at a higher level of vibration in unison with US. Love one another; do for others unselfishly, and take good care of yourself. Make time to meditate with US. Do these things and your vibrational level will rise to heights previously unknown.

What WE are telling you is that all is sacred and all of you understand spirit and soul. Look within yourselves and you shall see. You shall recognize that wonderful being and creator that you are. You shall see that all is connected and you don't need a few to tell you that, tell yourselves. There is no information of life and all it entails that each and every one of you is not privy to.

Remember this: You can! You will!

There is no way to not be pure spirit. Each of you is solely alive and functioning due to life force or spirit. Whomever among you that might be perceived to be evil, is still, as explained before, having their spirit influenced by spirits of a lower form or vibration. Remember, all is vibration. This means that the spirit of that person is at a low vibration. Thus, allowing a low vibration that is, shall WE say, a little higher than theirs to control or cause them to act in a way that is not for their highest good.

Further, some claim that to raise one's vibration, one must be baptized in water. Now WE already explained to you that you are mostly water. If this is the case, how could more water raise your vibrational level? Well it can't. Yet, more water, certainly higher pH water, can at certain levels assist your physical being in becoming healthier.

Therefore, WE reiterate that all are spiritual and all are divine as you understand the word to mean. It doesn't matter, if you believe it or not. Even if you were taught that you are sinful and going to the mythical place called "Hell," do not be discouraged. Whoever told you this, told you a lie. None of you are evil or wicked. Do not allow the self-righteous teachings of some power-hungry people to keep you from realizing who and what you really are. Visualize each and every one of your peers as a spiritual being on a spiritual quest. Remember, some of you, once again, have only made poor lower vibrational decisions in the past and of course can turn the page at any given time. WE promise you this.

Also remember that you do not have to go into isolation for long periods of time to raise your spirit. If you do choose to isolate yourself, make it of a short isolation. Go into one's self and come back out. Clear your mind, gather your thoughts, and get back into the human race. Remember, if you do not go within from time to time, you will go without. After quiet introspection one can function at a higher level of vibration, and thus, help others. Your life is the place to practice all that WE have given you in moments of solitude. Learn that detachment and separation from the masses is good to use once you interact with the masses. It can keep you safe in the midst of much lower vibrational activity.

WE LOVE YOU!

WE ARE SPIRIT AND SO ARE YOU,

FOR WE ARE YOU AND YOU ARE US.

Travel

Why do you think WE would give you information on this subject? Well, it is important. Yes, you may read of distant places and study different cultures in books. However, this is limiting you. There is nothing like experience; you know this, remember this. This is one of the reasons for racism and hatred on your home, your planet, your Earth. Many of you have allowed others to tell you what to think, what to think or perceive of other cultures, how they live and interact with each other. See for yourself.

You will begin to grasp the connection of all that is. You will begin to understand that there is no difference except location and acclimation from their ancestors and yours. You will understand more that adaptation to climate and region caused much, if not all, of the physical differences between you and your brothers and sisters. All of you have much in common. The blood that runs through you is the same, you breathe the same air, drink the same water, and eat the same foods. Peas in a pod you are; you will never be able to escape this fact no matter what you say or what you do. No matter how you try to formulate in your mind that somehow, someway, you are not connected to others on your home, your planet, your Earth.

WE highly suggest and put forth to you that it would be a very good idea, a revelation to you, to be an anthropologist. Did you know each of you is? Therefore, take trips and journeys outside your local area. There are many city dwellers that have never crossed a ten-block barrier. There are many rural folks who have only been to small cities and, thus, limit themselves to images and concepts of big cities as seen on the television. There are millions of you who do not even take a walk to get to know your neighbor two houses down the street. And you wonder why you can't get along with others or have no friends. Sad, WE must say. Further, it is unnecessary and limiting to the individual. However, it will get better. WE know it will.

There are countless numbers of you who will say this is elementary information and there is nothing new about it. However, if you do, you will only be sending out your negative self into the universe. For, there are many that do not know this. There are many who have never been told to get out and see the world or even the cities or towns twenty miles north, south, east, or even west of you.

Thus, WE put this request out to you each of you and, if it does not apply, let it fly. (Smile) Visit other places, states, and countries. See the world, for it's your world! Visit the south of France, the Mediterranean, and the Pyramids. See what man has done with the Golden Gate Bridge, the Great Wall of China, and the Taj Mahal. Why not go to the Coliseum in Rome or the American Grand Canyon? All over your globe there are places to go and people to see.

Taking a trip widens your perspective. You can do it! Why not? This, of course, will raise the vibrational level of yourselves and others on your planet. Additionally, it will cause you to not be at the mercy of others telling you what to think or do. Or maybe you like being told what to think or do? WE hope not. If you do, it is time to stop and think for yourself. You are wonderful and capable of great things. Find out how wonderful the world in which you live is and become familiar with your others. Each and every one of you are CREATORS. Create an open mind and heart. WE love you!

Marriage

It is an institution you created. Thus, if you wish, honor it. WE do have two questions for you: (WE like to stir up your mental processes from time to time.)

- Do you believe marriage to be a good practice, as you understand the word good to be?

- And does it have to be legal, certified by a piece of paper?

You don't have to answer it now; think on it. Have group discussions about it.

In what you consider to be early times, when the thinking ability of man was advanced, one of you knew the moment you saw someone if this person was for you. This would even occur if the union considered was arranged by the parents or other arrangers.

Just one look into the eyes of another human tells each of you many things. If you look deeply, you will be able to fully understand and feel from your inner being if this one is good for you or not.

The question after this is:

- Will the two of you do what is necessary to maintain the relationship?

Each of you has the innate ability to work things out, to create success, if you so desire. Each one of you can support and defend the other in all sorts of situations, if you but wish to. You can, support and care for the one you love if they suffer from what you term "mental issues," if you but wish to.

WE are saying you have also created divorce to get out of doing the things that each of you stated you would do for the other. Therefore, it is not in the highest good for any of you to say to self that you can't continue in a relationship. You can! However, "is it in the highest good to continue the marriage in the face of that which any of you are no longer willing to do?"

WE tell you the decision is yours. Each of you, needs to answer to yourself. There are many of you that got out of a marriage only to find out later, that you should not have, or that, if you would have just hung in there a little longer, it may have worked out. Many of you have deep regrets after that other has sprung into a higher level of vibration later in life. WE need to add that WE are not speaking about a marriage in which one of you has fallen deeply under the influence of lower vibrations and may hurt themselves or the other. However, it could have just required giving that person some space to recognize and regain themselves.

Since you do have marriage, why would you create something and not honor it? If you can't honor it, then change it; conform it into what you desire it to be. And, you have changed it many times throughout human history. In recent times alone, many of you are waking up as individuals and as a society to see that you can't place restrictions on who can marry whom. Have you not learned yet that the more you tell people what they can't do they will do it? Why have you not accepted this? The reason people behave as they do is because each of you has free will. As WE explained to you before, you are free to do what you like, how you like. If it is not in your highest good, you know it, no one has to tell you.

It is now time to answer the question that many on your home, your planet, your Earth have. Should men marry men and women marry women? The answer is, "Why not?" As long as it harms not themselves or others, and remember, there is no judge except self on self. It is up to the individual. Who told you that one had to marry to be right in the eyes of US? Oh, WE forgot, the church did!

If you are to love and cherish the other, do so. If you are to marry and share life and joy with a person, do so. It is important to allow the space between you to cause you to come together. Pour each other's drink, but have your own cup, lest you or the other acquires resentments. Have your fun together. Dance and sing and make love as much as possible. Yet, once again, allow each other to be alone and with US. Walk side by side in a synchronized glide. Stand together, but not within each other's space. Remember, this is the way it should be.

Remember, if you desire not to marry, then don't. It is that simple. No one can force you, for you have free will. It is better for you to be alone or in many, what you call, "sexual relationships," if you refuse to honor what you together as a society have created.

However, if you choose the latter, respect yourself and the other or others. If you think you cannot do this, or come to a point where you know you can't do it, Stop!

YOU HAVE THE POWER, REMEMBER!

JUDGMENTS

There is no right or wrong, except in your mind. Each of you will make decisions not conducive with your highest self during the course of a lifetime. Each of you will make decisions not taking into account the highest good for others. All of you are connected. This is, how it is. None of you can do anything that does not affect the other. So, as you make choices each day, ponder upon this fact. None of you can do anything which is hidden from all. For as one of you commits what you have deemed as a crime, all of you created or allowed it to be. You created it together by allowing the situations and circumstances agreeable for it to exist. Each of you fully understands this on a spiritual level. Many of you do not wish to understand it on a conceptual level.

Man's written laws are just that; written by man, and changed whenever you decide to change them. What was appropriate yesterday may not be tomorrow. Therefore, be careful as you sling around contempt and judgments. Some will come back to bite you; many of your kind have firsthand experience with this notion. Keep in mind that you created your court systems as they stand. Take a look at them; scrutinize them and adjust them as to what you desire them to be. Your laws were created by you, for you. Those which you know are unfair to others should be changed or done away with. But you already know this. Remember!

Therefore, eliminate the situations and circumstances that allow such acts as murder and injustice to thrive and such will disappear. Remember, if you judge, you are in fact judging yourself. Yet, still, this is what you have created it to be. You can change it, if you but desire to do so. Try!

Acts of Compassion or Giving

You are one with all. There is no higher calling for any of you than helping others. WE placed this in you. Thus, remember, when you give to others, you give to yourself. You cannot keep what you have without giving some away. Thus, give to those less fortunate than yourself. Even the greediest of you gives at times for he or she basically understands that to keep receiving what he or she has, he or she must give away. If each of you gives more, more will you have, as will others. If all of you have, then wars and famines and the like will pass away. You are your brother's and sister's keeper, like it or not, for he or she is you.

This is a law of the universe as you understand it to be; you cannot change it. Therefore, flow with it. If one of you decides to go against the flow of life, you will reap as you sow. Know also that if one of you does not give, the selfishness of yourself will consume you, and, of course, cause undo and unnecessary lifetimes in the physical form. Further, remember there is no suffering in giving. WE do not know, or WE do know, where this line of thinking and behavior came from. Denying yourself of life's pleasures and joys to give to others is a most, as you call it, "ridiculous" idea. It causes inner turmoil that is unnecessary. Remember, light and love you are!

Remember!

Work

What is work, but the consuming of, what you call, "time"? You have devised it. You have set the parameters. Use this task you call "work" to uplift your life conditions on your home, your planet, your Earth, and the conditions of others. If you have this mind set, the consciousness of your planet shall be lifted, and joy and peace will ensue. It is up to only you to decide what you wish or desire to consume your time. Please, cause it to be something that you enjoy; something that will lift or raise your vibrational level. Whatever it is, do the best you can. This brings about satisfaction and peace of mind, you will feel better of yourself, your world, and others. You deserve the best, have it.

Remember!

Opposites

You in your present physical form will not be able to know or to experience anything without the opposite of that which you experience as existing. Know and Remember this. You created this. You could not understand being healthy, if you knew not pain. If you knew not cold, you would or could not understand hot or any other of the opposites that you have created to understand Who and What you are in your relative place in what you understand the universe to be. You must fully understand this simple law of the known universe, and, that its understanding will cause a certain rebirthing of your attitude within your being. This will cause a joy to spring from what you know as your soul and you will begin to cherish all on your Earth. This, by the way, is how it is supposed to be.

Remember!

Freedom

If WE could be sad, WE would be sad over the idea of this word. The conditions that you on your home, your planet, your Earth, have created, allowed the conception of this word. This would make US sad. For, it is very important for each of you to remember that all are free. There is nothing to discuss. What is needed to be discussed about this? All is spirit and one never will be able to contain the spirit. The spirit has no bounds. No chains or locks or prisons, devised by man, can or ever will be able to quash it. Therefore, know that the word itself was created by you, which causes the word itself not to come into itself. Remember, what you resist persists.

Remember and know.

This is the reason that throughout, what you call, "time," each time one of you or a group of you has tried to contain others, for whatever reasons, in servitude, sooner or later it has failed. For, the mass consciousness, sometimes, is slow to act. This, of course, is a result of the split. However, remembrance of this fact returns quickly to many and, of course, they have and always will start the ball rolling to correct this injustice. Also, remember it is only those, who for reasons only known to themselves and US, have allowed their vibrational levels to be lowered to a dangerous point which allows themselves to even come up with the idea of making others of their own kind slaves. Thus, they end up making themselves slaves to a foolishness of the worst sort.

Remember!

Time

You have created on your home, your planet and your Earth, what you must do for yourself. You needed or thought you desired something to place yourselves in order. This is because the universe is order, and WE are order. However, due to the forgetfulness, brought about by the split, you did not remember much order. Therefore, within your logical mind you created systems to cause you to feel as if you had some order about yourselves. Thus, you created, one of these systems and called, it "time" as you thought you should.

Yet, know you this! You have set forth into place a measure on that which is immeasurable. All exist together, all at once and forever. You do not have to remember this now, it is not time (smile) yet. What you have named, "yesterday" or the "past" is now or the present, which leads to the tomorrow, which is now. Time is a Space Continuum and not one at the same time (smile), and because of the split, you do not remember this. In order to understand what you have caused time to be, you must look at some of your concepts of it.

First and foremost, many of you feel there is not enough of it. Women speak of their biological clocks running out in regards to reproduction. In reality, certain reproductive actions are supposed to stop at a certain time, and of course, bodily cycles such as menopause have been accelerated or begin before they naturally should. This change in the reproduction system of the female body is due to many of your dietary and environmental concerns.

However, on Earth, things are changing or going back to the intended time frames, as you understand time frames to be; women are having children later in life now. Why? Well, you have been given certain technology by US and many women are eating better and taking better care of their bodies.

Men speak of not having all the hours needed in, what you call, "a day." And, if one of you dies, you say his or her time ran out. WE will tell you the truth; you have all the time you need. There is no need really to rush around and stress out over not completing a so-called "task." You should remember that things get done when they get done, and all the rushing does not help the process of completion. These actions may, in fact, harm it.

As told to you previously, the biology of your body has changed due to the split. At one time you lived for hundreds of years. Due to many of the activities chosen during man's history, life spans shortened somewhat. The good news, however, is that man's life span is increasing again. Take a look at medical studies; you can see the facts for yourselves. WE point out that you can turn back the hands of time on your aging process. Unfortunately, that information is for the next book. You can only digest so much at one time as it stands now.

Those in Physics will inform you that all time, as you understand it to be, exists equally, at one time. You have constructed the past, present, and future within your conscious mind. You have created photo albums to savor what you think the past is. You have invented the alarm clock and other time-keeping devices. You have calendars and schedules to tell you where to go and when to be there. This time management of yours is what you think you need, so be it. You have given yourself productivity charts and pay people to advise you on such. Therefore, if you feel you need someone to tell you what you intuitively already know, that's okay, too. You can successfully do all you wish or desire to do within, what you call, a "day." Moreover, each day you act in the highest good for yourself and others, you have wasted no time.

WE tell you time is vertical and, therefore, it cannot be horizontal. Moreover, everything that ever happened in your mind occurred on top of what is occurring and what will occur. But guess what? It is also reversed. You can go either way, back to the past or into the future. However, there is only "now," which, by the way, is forever. Again you need not ponder, worry, or stress too much of this matter now. It will come to remembrance for all of you later.

YOU WILL REMEMBER!

IX

Other Planets, Galaxies, and the Inhabitants

What is out there?
I looked into the starry night.
I wondered what's beyond my sight.
How distant are the stars from me?
How deep really is the deep blue sea?
What nocturnal mammals might there be?
Do I really care; do I really want to see?
What's on the other side of life?
Are there bills, do we have a wife?
Is there evolution of pollution?
Are abortions committed to end life?
Are there tubes connected to sustain one's life?
Do Mars men use a big bowie knife?
Do they have an IPod like me?
I wonder if they are looking down at me.
Do they look at me with a frown?
Do they shake their heads and point
down at the earthly clowns?
I wonder if I'll ever see those other beings
looking down at me!

WE have saved this for last. And WE have a question for you:

Do you really think that you are the only ones, WE mean, beings that function and live life?

Well, you are not the only ones. There are other creators on other planets. Some are like you, others are not. Some of their civilizations are behind you in evolution and some are far, far, more advanced in what you on your home, your planet, and your Earth, call technology.

There are also those on or in other planes of existence. What WE are saying is that some of them, like US, have no form as you understand form to be. They are gases and clouds so to speak. They travel at the speed of light and sound as WE do. And they have visited your plane of existence.

However, like you, they are not in full remembrance and are not integrated back into US. They do not worry as you understand worrying to be. They do have certain tasks to complete, to remember, before they are with US, as do many of you. There are those elsewhere or in other planes of existence just like you. There are planets which house societies such as yours. However, they are not in your universe. They, the beings that live there, are learning about themselves and how to reach a higher vibrational level of consciousness as are you. They have material interests as do you. They are ingenious as are you. They have developed hierarchies and sub-cultures as have you, and will, as you will sooner or later, come to the conclusion that pecking-order systems are not of a high vibration. They will come to the realization, as will you, that WE are all one.

These civilizations are heterosexual, bi-sexual, and homosexual, as are you. They categorize items in somewhat the same manner as you on Earth. They seek profit and gain, measure loss, hate, and do not really care of what will come of their environment until it is perhaps too late. They love and, as you have, what WE term, a "heterodox" opinion of self. They, like many of you, seek to understand all that there is, and like many of you, refuse to look inside to see that you are All there is. These also build what you understand to be corporations and are trying to venture out into their known universe as are you.

There are also those on other planets in other galaxies who are totally mentally, optically, and spiritually evolved. They move objects with their minds and have very little use, if any, for what you have termed, a "body." They see each other through time and space and send each other love and light all day long. They have things to remember before they return to US, as do you. They have visited your planet before and given technological information to many of you throughout, what you call, "time." They are of what you may term a "technocratic" or "technocracy" society. They do not worry or ponder on anything other than the production of what they need to continue to function as a society.

Now, if you look at the historical evidence of your home, your planet, your Earth, you will see signs of past advanced civilizations. Investigate Sumerian history and the hieroglyphic paintings in caves and walls of Europe and South America, i.e., not to mention the findings in Africa and other locations on Earth. Earlier WE spoke of Mesopotamia. Also, there were the Babylonians, all whom received information from higher vibrational beings. Were there places in your world's past called "Lemuria" and "Atlantis?" Yes! Were they and the Mayan and other ancient civilizations destroyed by the ones from whom they received information? No! Did they create their own destruction by not adhering to the pleas of US whom came in a different form to help you elevate your selves? Yes! These, as you call them, "people" did not follow the teachings of being humane to all, not to be greedy or lust for power. Will you take and learn from their misguided decisions? Yes, you will, for WE will help you remember!

Throughout time you have pictured the Lemurians to have white long hair. Some of them did, but not all. Were they giants? No. Are there Crystal Skulls? Yes, and some other kinds, too, that will be discovered soon. Remember, WE told you this! WE will touch upon this in the next book also. Where do you think the technology for the building of, what you call, the "Great Pyramids" came from? US. WE also gave Frank Lloyd Wright his inspiration. The creation of tools, used by early man, and the idea for Stonehenge, came from what you understand to be spacemen, US, and, technically, you. There are many more marvels to come. WE love you. WE speak to you of this for it is crucial for the remembrance process. You must grasp how the first civilizations in Europe evolved.

You must understand the actual evolution of the concepts presented to you by early religions. Most, if not all of them, came from an attempt to cover our earthly assistance to mankind. There are those who wished and desired to take credit where credit was not due. If you check into and look deep into the recorded historical statements of those on your home, your planet, your Earth, that have made great contributions to your history you will find the following: They have all acknowledged All there is, was, and ever shall be, as their inspiration. Why? Because they all knew from whence their help cometh and they were acting out of a high vibrational level and desired for all to know.

This is the reason that none of you should take astronomy, astrology, numerology, or channeling lightly. Treat it as you would mathematics or science. It is all for you, for your learning and elevation of spirit. However, remember if it is not for your highest good or speaks towards negative outcomes and actions, flee from it as you would flee from the lava of a volcano. Our son, Carl Sagan, knew of the wonders from US. He spent many years passing on knowledge from, what you call, "above." Know that there are many more doing the same. All out there in, what you call, "space" have given you the processes to make telescopes and rocket ships. Your physics laws of quantum theory and the constraints of the universe come from US and your brothers and sisters who care deeply about the conditions on your planet. You, too, will reach others in the galaxy and give them information. They, too, will think you are Gods. Will you tell them you are just like them in a different form, as the Mayans were told, but did not listen? They and others chose to worship others instead of themselves.

All advanced civilizations have been able to control their natural resources. Your home is working on it now. This is another sign of the raising of vibrational level on your planet. They can control the weather as you will be able to also accomplish, if you but try. You are learning to tap the power of, what you call, your "sun" for the advancement of your species. Yes, you will colonize other planets. All in your science fiction will become science fact. Do not you feel this? What you understand as time and space can and will be controlled and manipulated by man. Will you use this knowledge wisely? These are the questions you must ask yourself and each other. The Time is Now! The time will come when you will no longer need nor desire to use oil and coal as you do now. This in itself will alleviate many poor conditions on your home, your planet, your Earth. WE tell you and assure you that your Earth will be much greater than it already is before you come back to US. It is a part of the process, the remembering process. You will harness the power of black holes and supernovae. Mark OUR words.

WE LOVE YOU SO VERY MUCH.

YOU ARE US.

Now wrap your mind around this. Previously, WE informed you that some of you have been on other planes of existence. Many of you lived, as you call it, on some of the aforementioned places. You did not fully fulfill your contract and returned to another plane to learn more of the nature of self and the WE. You also entered your new plane to teach things to those on your current plane of existence of what you remember from a previous life. Think you not that many of you living today and those that were alive before did not live on and in another plane of existence before? You would be in denial and, in fact, fooling yourselves.

It is all true.

Therefore, if you are one of those who remembers a previous life, share what you know with those who are on a high vibrational level for now. Allow the light and love you remember to shine upon your fellow man on Earth. Give the information to your world to help and assist it in obtaining its highest vibrational level possible. Do you really think, for one moment, that Jesus, Mark Twain, Kahlil Gibran, Thomas Edison, Benjamin Franklin, and others throughout time did not share with you what they learned on some other plane with mankind? You need to understand that much of your music, art, and literature as you understand it, was given to you from the higher selves of others in remembrance of who and what they were and are. The time will come when they and you will be fully understood. The time is closer than you think.

Controversial material some of you may think.
Mind blowing?
No, once again just the truth!
Remember, Who you are!

Remember!

You stand today, as you understand today, to be at a crossroad. What will you do? Will you pass this information off as, unreal or untrue? What will you do? Will you remember Who you are? Will you begin to uplift yourself? Will you begin to live these words and reap the benefits? You, your home, your planet, your Earth, all stand at the crossroad. There is the high road and there is the low.

Which way will you go?

Conclusion

The writer of this book and his wife have taken much from those just like them — humans, pieces of US, who do not believe the things they are saying. They find it hard to believe, that WE speak to each of you. They find it hard to believe the facts that all came from US, All there is, was, and ever shall be. They find it hard to believe that you can have your heart's desires, if it is in your highest good. Therefore, they have been ridiculed, slandered, labeled crazy, called blasphemers, devils, and sinners.

This book you are reading now was rejected many times. The writer of these words is not the author; WE are. He was told that the information did not fit the current theme of many of the publishers on your home, your planet, your Earth, who by their own admission "put out" spiritual or new age materials for the masses. They were told by some of these publishers, who had published books similar to this one, that they did not take channeled materials anymore, when the truth is that all any of you do which is for the enjoyment, advancement, or raising of the vibrational level of your kind is channeled. WE know that the rejections or skepticism to accept the manuscript was what you would term as hypocritical, phony, or not genuine. In truth, they just did not really take a good clear look at the words. That's okay, too; for once again all of you have freedom of choice. That is our greatest gift to you.

Please understand that WE fully understood that this book would not be published until the right vibrational level was in place with all involved. The writer and his wife will again be called names by those subject to lower vibrational influences.

WE wish to tell you, as many of you well know, that in the past just being called "SINNER" has caused many of your kind to commit suicide. WE wonder, even though WE know the answer, if those who created and use the word "sinner" so often, and descriptive words like it, to classify one of their own, think they are on a high vibration? What do you think? Even family members who claim love, said they loved them, could or would not support them in their claims of speaking to US, the very thing that all of you say you hope for, to speak or have a personal conversation with US. Even still, many of you refuse to admit this fact; it's okay. WE know the truth and so do you. This is a strange concept. Strange, considering that most of you make an attempt to speak to US in, what you call, "prayers."

At any rate, they, as all who have raised their vibrational levels, became and become subject to attacks from lower vibrations. That is the way it is! Or, may WE again quote a song inspired by US, "That's the Way of the World." Know that WE prepared them for it. WE, as WE do with all of you many times, gave them the inner strength to persevere the tricks and games of lower vibrational portions or pieces of US. WE gave them knowledge to sustain themselves as WE do with all of you. Many of you understand this, for you have had to stand against lower vibrations in your daily life. WE gave and give you, too, the remembrance that Love overcomes all; Love always has and always will win.

All of you pray for, hope, and dream of having your remembrance awakened. It is instilled within you and it is happening now. The remembrance is occurring through the writings you have just read. WE are giving you through the writer, and through others at this time, remembrance. However, each day you live what you understand life to be, you give your sacred self all the answers you need. Each time any of you look at any portion of your universe, WE are there. Even the things you take for granted, such as the weaving in the rug you may be standing on. Look at it; some of you or one of you created it. Thus, WE created it. Do you still, yet not see? Everything around you gives, each of you, if you look, remembrance of whom and what you are — whom and what WE are. Because of this book, many of you are listening more to your higher self and it is what you may term as "good."

WE will always help you. You are beginning to feel our assistance; you are in the process now. You are recalling just how powerful your mind is. Once any of you or all of you takes hold of these wonderful universal truths, you will propel yourself a bit closer to US. And, in fact, many have already begun to do so. More and more of you are working towards a cleaner Earth. You are eating healthier. Many of you are taking better care of yourselves. This is occurring on your Earth in far greater numbers than before. It is, of course, the way WE planned it. It is the way you planned it long ago and far away from what you understand reality now to be.

WE are happy. WE are joyous because you are coming back to US. You are becoming happier, too. WE love you. More of you are starting to love yourself. It is wonderful, is it not? You are praying more, talking to US more. You are taking more time for deep reflection of self which brings you closer to US. You are beginning to treat each other better and it is, simply, a result of your treating yourselves better. Yes, WE are happy that the mass consciousness is rising. The dialogue has begun. Watch your TV shows, listen to your radios, listen and watch in the coffee shops across the world. Many are talking of what WE speak. Many are remembering things that only come from US, things of Light and Love, Hope and Joy. They are remembering the Here and the Now, the When and the Where. They are coming to fully understand and discern that all is connected; that All, is All there is, was, and ever shall be.

WILL YOU REMEMBER?

WILL YOU REMEMBER US?

WILL YOU REMEMBER YOU?

WE WILL SEE! ALL WILL SEE.

WE LOVE YOU!

REMEMBER!

WE WILL SPEAK WITH YOU SOON; LISTEN!